How To Handle A Bully

Susanna Palomares
Dianne Schilling

Cover Design — Linda Jean Thille
Original Illustratoions — Jan Stone

Copyright © 2020, Innerchoice Publishing • All rights reserved
ISBN - 10: 1-56499-100-8
ISBN - 13: 978-1-56499-100-3

INNERCHOICE PUBLISHING
15079 Oak Chase Court
Wellington, FL 33414
(561) 790-0132 • Email: info@InnerchoicePublishing.com
www.innerchoicepublishing.com

All rights reserved. Activity sheets may be reproduced in quantities sufficient for distribution to students in classrooms and other programs utilizing How To Handle A Bully. All other reproduction by any mechanical, photographic, or electronic process, by any other means, or in the form of a photographic or digital recording is expressly prohibited without the written permission of the publisher. Nor may it be stored in a retrieval system, transmitted or otherwise copied for public or private use without such written permission. Requests for such permission should be directed to INNERCHOICE PUBLISHING.

Dedication

For Marika Schilling, who invented many creative strategies for dealing with the bullies in her life — and prevailed.

Contents

The Basics of Bully Prevention	9
How to Use the Activities	21
How to Lead a Sharing Circle	23
Sharing Circle Rules	28

Activities and Experience Sheets

What Is Bully Behavior?	31
Bullies, Targets, Bystanders, and Upstanders	35
Why Do Bullies Bully?	43
Asking for Help	46
Speaking Out Against Bullying	50
How to Avoid a Bully	53
New-Kid Welcome Kits	57
What I Like and Respect About Me	60
Positive Self-Talk	62
Creating Positive Affirmations	65
What's Your Style? Aggressive, Passive or Assertive	68
Developing Listening Skills	74
Relaxation and Anger Management Strategies	78
Reach for the Sky – Developing Confident Behaviors	83
Say No, Then Go	87
A Book of Kindness	90
Two Sides of Friendship	92
Setting Friendship Goals	95

6

No Room for Bullies — 99
Bringing It All Together — 102

Sharing Circle Topics

Something About Me That You Wouldn't Know Unless I Told You — 107
Someone Tried to Make Me Do Something I Didn't Want to Do — 108
How Someone Made Me Feel Like Part of the Group — 109
A Time I Was Rejected Because Something About Me Was Different — 110
A Time I Felt Left Out — 111
I Did Something That Made Me Feel Like a Good Person — 112
A Time I Felt Anger and Handled It Well — 113
A Way I Show I'm a Good Friend — 114
A Friend I Have Who Is Different From Me — 115
Something Nice I Did For a Friend — 116
I Told Someone How I Was Feeling — 117
A Time I Listened Well to Someone — 118
How I Let Others Know I'm Interested In What They Say — 119
Something About Me That's Likable and Worthy of Respect — 120
How I Show Respect Toward Others — 121
What's Good and Bad About Peer Pressure — 122
A Time I Stood Up for What Was Right — 123
I Stopped Myself from Damaging Someone's Property — 124
Someone Who Trusts Me — 125
Someone I Would Like to Know Better — 126
Something I Like About Myself Right Now — 127
It Made Me Feel Good to Make Someone Else Feel Good — 128
How Somebody Hurt My Feelings — 129
I Could Have Hurt Someone's Feelings, But I Didn't — 130
A Time I Stood Up for Something I Strongly Believe In — 131

The Basics of Bully Prevention

Adam dreaded physical education. Smaller and less developed than the other boys, he lacked athletic skill, which earned him a daily barrage of shoves, jeers and threats from Kevin, the class hulk. On the big, open playing field, Adam could neither hide his awkwardness nor "disappear" as he had learned to do almost everywhere else on the school grounds. Talking back to Kevin only fueled his tormentor's contempt and, since the coach either didn't notice or didn't care, Adam coped by skipping school as often as possible or getting excused from gym for phony injuries.

Donald and Rudy were rivals in their neighborhood — no one was ever sure why. Maybe it was because their respective families were always arguing about parking spaces, noise levels and yard maintenance. Whatever the reason, the boys didn't like each other and frequently ended up in fights, even at school. Both were big for the 5th grade and both had a group of staunch supporters, so their skirmishes usually drew crowds. Even kids who weren't involved seemed compelled to watch, and there was much calculating and betting about who would win each bout.

Which of these stories involves bullying? Only Adam's. While regrettable, the ongoing fights between Donald and Rudy are examples of poorly managed conflict, not bullying.

What Is Bullying?

Bullying is a pattern of repeated, intentionally cruel behavior. It differs from normal peer conflict in a number of ways.

- Power. Bullies are almost always more powerful that their targets — bigger, stronger, older, or just tougher. Adam was small for his age, Kevin husky. Donald and Rudy were equally matched — similar in both age and size.
- Support. Bullies choose targets in part for their relative isolation. Alone and exposed, Adam was an easy target, whereas Donald and Rudy both had staunch support groups.
- Vulnerability. Bullies look for potential targets among the weak. A child who is sensitive and seemingly without defense is seen as easy prey.

- Intensity and duration. Bullying is rarely a one-time occurrence. Adam was subject to Kevin's barrage of bullying every time he showed up for P.E.
- Intent to harm. Bullies are sadistic. They gain release and satisfaction from hurting their targets. They enjoy watching the pain they cause.

Bullying can be anything from teasing to physical aggression. It can be physical, emotional, psychological or sexual. It can be as overt as a punch in the ribs or as seemingly innocuous as a verbal put-down. The important thing is not the specific action, but the intent with which the action is delivered and the effect on the target. The goal of a bully is to do damage. The target's pain, anger and humiliation are proof that damage has been done.

Bullying is certainly not new, though concern over bullying, and the proliferation of bully-prevention programs, are relatively recent phenomena. Alarming increases in school violence have prompted many educators to regard bully behavior in the elementary grades as a prelude to more serious problems in middle school and beyond. Bullying is a form of harassment, a range of behaviors to which our society has become increasingly sensitized in recent years.

What Is Cyberbullying

With the growth of technology the ability and incidence of cyberbullying has increased. Online bullying can be anything that gets posted online and is designed to hurt, threaten, intimidate, or embarrass another person. It can include photos, messages, or pages that are not removed when the individual who posted them has been asked to do so. Often cyberbullying is an anonymous act and can be carried out by an individual or a group. Like in person bullying, cyberbullying is repeated over time.

Why Do Kids Bully?

Like most behavior patterns, bullying is learned. Genetics may predispose a child to be big and strong, but only experience teaches him to be aggressive and hostile.

At home, a bully may receive physical punishment for real or perceived misbehavior. A child who is spanked, slapped or beaten into submission learns to use these same methods to control others.

Children who witness repeated acts of intolerance, force and bullying among family members are likely to adopt the prejudices and coercive behaviors that appear to work for those closest to them. When they come to school, they assume that the same rules apply.

For reasons already mentioned (parental abuse, poor modeling), bullies may come to school heavily burdened with feelings of frustration, anger and self-loathing. If aggression is the norm at home, some will find a way to strike out at school, usually picking convenient, passive targets.

Finally, for all their show of power, many people believe that bullies are weak where it counts most — inside. Common sense tells us that a child who likes and respects herself can be expected to treat others with caring and consideration. If she bullies, it is because she has low self-esteem and needs to pick on vulnerable peers in order to feel better about herself. This is no doubt true in many cases, however, a number of experts argue that just the opposite can be true — that, deserved or not, some bullies actually have pretty high self-esteem.

How Widespread Is Bullying?

Bullying occurs everywhere — in homes, neighborhoods, schools, workplaces, shopping malls, the military, and government. In person or online, children who are bullied by their parents may try to dominate weaker peers at school. Years later, they may be using bully tactics to gain advantages and win promotions at work.

A lot of otherwise reasonable people become bullies behind the wheel of a car. Witness the hotshot who rips a right turn just as you step off the curb into the crosswalk, or the driver who'd sooner run a car off the road than allow anyone to merge ahead of him in traffic.

By some estimates, 75 percent of children will be bullied at some point in their school career. Incidents of bullying appear first in preschool, gradually increase throughout the elementary grades, peak in middle school and decline in high school.

In the elementary grades, bullying may be confined to teasing, name-calling and other put-downs. As they grow older, confirmed bullies are apt to resort to increasingly physical and violent behavior.

The warning signs for bullying are well known. If you know what to look for, you can identify most bullies early in their careers, and early in the school year at every grade level.

The Consequences of Bullying

A single incidence of bullying, during recess for example, impacts everyone in the immediate environment and trickles down from there. The target, if she returns to class at all, probably does so in a state of extreme anxiety, anger or humiliation. She may lash out at other children or distract them with her obvious suffering. Bystanders return to class with feelings ranging from excitement to guilt. Everyone has difficulty concentrating and the learning environment is poisoned.

In addition to demoralizing the school community and contributing to a negative learning environment, bullying has specific, predictable effects on targets, bystanders and bullies.

- Effects on the Target. Children will go to great lengths to avoid being bullied. If they don't know positive, constructive ways of protecting themselves they will use negative, destructive ways. Cutting classes and feigning illness in order to stay home are common solutions. Unless countered by parents or other adults, such tactics can lead to chronic truancy and, later, dropping out of school entirely.

  Targets of repeated bullying often become socially isolated. Marked by the stigma of constant humiliation, they have difficulty making friends. Other kids avoid them. Lonely and ostracized, they fail to learn peer-accepted social skills and may use eccentric, "weird" behaviors to attract friends, further undermining their efforts to fit in and be liked.

  Anxiety and dread are the target's constant companions. When fear and suffering become habitual, a "target mentality" may be locked in for life. Only a few years separate the bullied child from the adult misfit who blames himself and everyone else for an endless succession of problems that somehow defy resolution.

  Bullied children often become deeply depressed. They have difficulty learning, and their grades suffer. A few will eventually choose suicide. Cyberbullying cases leading to suicide of targets have made news headlines in recent years. Others — those who are raging inside — may retaliate in ways that are shocking and unexpected even to themselves.

- Effects on the Bystander. Bullies love an audience, and most have no trouble attracting one. It's normal human behavior to want to gauge the strength of a potential foe, which may account in part for the tendency of children to watch bully encounters. On some level, observers are probably wondering what they would do if the bully turned on them. Some may actually be engaged in a kind of mental rehearsal.

    In addition to rapt fascination, bystanders often feel uncertain how to act, helpless to intervene, and (later) guilty for not having come to the aid of the target. A vocal minority of bystanders may become excited by the entertainment value of the bullying event and use cheers and taunts to incite further harassment or violence.

    Another way many bystanders are affected is by having their freedom of association curtailed. A bully who has prestige and power can make social outcasts of the children she bullies. Bystanders may hesitate to associate with the target for fear of losing status or becoming the bully's next prey.

- Effects on the Bully. If a bully is masking feelings of worthlessness and low self-esteem, every bullying act is likely to deepen his self-contempt. This may prompt him to bully even more relentlessly to strengthen his cover. Most of his classmates will start to avoid him, either out of fear or because they simply don't like his antisocial behavior. Bullies are significantly more likely than non-bullies to be convicted of a crime by the time they reach early adulthood. Children who become bullies often remain bullies for life. They batter their wives, abuse their children, and produce another generation of bullies. They develop few lasting friendships, have problems at work, and frequently end up in prison.

    The bullies you see around you at school are not merely facing poor grades and disciplinary problems, they are facing a lifetime of trouble.

Finally, any of these effects if experienced often enough can interfere with learning. Uneasy, frightened, guilt-ridden children seldom make good students.

Boys and Girls Bully Differently

Most adults, when they think of a schoolyard bully, picture an aggressive, belligerent male — hulky and maybe even a bit cloddish. That stereotype still plays out reliably in movies and cartoons and, to some extent, in real life. Boys who bully are usually bigger than their peers, enjoy using their power, are boastful, blaming, antisocial and relatively low in emotional intelligence.

No comparable stereotype exists for the female bully, yet girls do bully — often. The methods used by female bullies are far more subtle, which is probably why female bullies don't readily conform to a particular image.

While male bullies prefer direct, physical, one-to-one encounters, female bullies favor social exclusion, manipulation, rumor mills, and bullying in groups. Their behavior, though not often physically threatening, is marked by a special kind of cruelty.

Identifying Bullies — and Bully Candidates

Most kids occasionally participate in some form of bullying. They may not physically harm or intimidate another child, but they engage in teasing, heckling, put-downs, social exclusion, or some other form of psychological/emotional bullying.

Despite these occasional cruel acts, most children are not dedicated bullies. Those who are — or who have the potential to be — can often be identified by the traits and behaviors they exhibit. The typical bully:

- Lacks empathy, compassion and concern for the feelings of others.
- Is larger and/or stronger than peers.
- Manipulates and uses others to achieve ends.
- Is bossy and controlling; likes to dominate others.
- Lacks social skills; may be antisocial.
- Uses teasing as a way of getting to know others.
- Enjoys feeling powerful, competent and in control.
- Craves attention; shows off and acts tough to get it.
- Lacks empathy for targets.
- Gets pleasure or satisfaction from seeing others suffer.
- Enjoys and frequently provokes conflict.
- Lacks guilt; shows no remorse.
- Blames the target. Insists that the target provoked the attack and deserves the consequences.
- Blames others for own problems; refuses to accept responsibility.
- Is defensive and guarded; believes in "getting them before they get me."

- Is easily offended by innocent actions and/or remarks.
- Lacks friends, or has a few close friends (followers/lieutenants).

Identifying Targets — and Target Candidates

The majority of children are targets of a bully at one time or another just by being in the wrong place at the wrong time. Only a few, however, become the object of repeated attacks. According to student surveys, kids who don't "fit in" are the bully's number one targets. Not fitting in usually means that a child is different in some way. Whether awkward, oddly (or poorly) dressed, extremely tall, short, skinny, fat, or are of a different race or religion, targets have difficulty assimilating within the peer culture.

Out of fear or shame, many targets keep incidents of bullying secret. Visions of clumsy interventions on the part of teachers or parents may be enough to silence them. Why make the situation worse by telling an adult? Targets may also fear retribution (from the bully) or further ostracism (from peers). Vigilance is needed to identify targets. Take note if any child is:

- Frequently disheveled (torn clothing, cuts, scrapes, bruises)
- Missing money, belongings, lunch.
- Socially isolated.
- Perceived by peers to be different (features, body type, clothes, actions, speech, race, religion).
- Socially inept; doesn't know the "social ropes."
- Emotional (cries, clings)
- Extremely shy, timid, sensitive.
- Nervous, anxious, fearful.
- Withdrawn, sullen, depressed.
- Physically smaller or weaker than peers.
- Frequently absent from school.
- Frequently ill or voices numerous physical complaints
- Has a physical/medical disability
- Lacking healthy self-esteem or self-image
- Failing or performing poorly in school.
- Not interested in school.

What You Can Do?

As a concerned adult, parent, or professional educator, you are probably already doing much to prevent and deal with bullying in your own setting. The fact that you are reading this book indicates that you want to do more.

- Start with Policy. It is crucial to develop clear and effective school policy for preventing bullying and effectively dealing with it when it occurs. Once a course of action has been formulated and agreed upon, everyone needs to be informed about exactly what the policy is. Tips for policy development include:
    - Build on existing discipline guidelines.
    - Apply the policy consistently.
    - Enlist everyone's commitment.
    - Establish procedures for investigating reported incidences of bullying.
    - Adequately monitor hot spots where bullying is likely to take place.
    - Respond quickly and consistently to any bullying incident.
    - Immediately step in and help any child who is bullied.

- Raise Awareness. All members of the school community — teachers, counselors, administrators, students, parents and support personnel — need to learn what bullying is, how it affects the community, and what they can do to prevent or stop it. Tips for raising awareness include:
    - Work with students and adults to determine the extent of bullying in your setting.
    - To obtain current data, conduct a survey. Share the results with everyone.
    - Hold classroom discussions.
    - Adopt one or more curricular programs aimed at preventing/reducing bullying.
    - Teach parents how they can help.

- Enlist Everyone in the Effort. Make it clear that prevention of bullying is everyone's business. Make it a school-wide, yearlong effort. Tips include:
    - Mobilize all students, including those who are neither targets nor bullies. Teach them how to react when they witness acts of bullying (how to be an upstander).
    - Make it safe for kids to report bullying. Protect anonymity.
    - Develop peer mediation programs to help students deal more effectively with conflict.

— Encourage kids to talk about bullying in general, as well as to report specific instances of bullying.
— Never trivialize the problem or make excuses for a kid who bullies.

- Create a Positive School/Classroom Climate. The biggest part of prevention is creating an environment where bullying cannot easily flourish. Tips include:
  — Help kids develop positive social skills, including conflict management skills.
  — Develop programs that provide recognition, admiration and respect for positive, pro-social behaviors.
  — Avoid giving attention to the negative behaviors of bullies.
  — Reward and celebrate helpfulness, friendliness, kindness, honesty, responsibility, positive leadership, and other desirable character traits.
  — Be open and honest in your own communications. Set an example by talking openly about your own experiences, feelings, values and concerns.
  — Strengthen the resistance of all students to bully behaviors through systematic efforts to promote healthy social-emotional development in every child.

Helping Targets Cope More Effectively

All children can benefit from learning strategies and skills for dealing with bullies. If you have an opportunity to identify and work with individual targets, so much the better. Many of the same techniques can be reinforced through one-to-one interaction. Even role-play — a powerful way for children to practice and internalize new behaviors — can often be accomplished very effectively in individual counseling or teaching sessions.

Targets need to develop a thoroughgoing awareness of what precipitates a typical bully encounter; what they do (or don't do) to contribute to the situation; their feelings before, during and after an encounter; and what's in it for the bully.

Once a foundation of awareness is developed, help targets learn techniques and skills for deflecting and neutralizing bully attacks. Targets can learn ways to avoid being an easy target. They can test new ways of standing, walking, talking and relating to others. Reading about or discussing behavior change is just the beginning, however. Some form of behavioral rehearsal is essential. Skits, role plays or simply repeating aloud new ways of responding are helpful.

Involve the parents of targets as early as possible in the process so that they can reinforce your efforts. Offer specific suggestions, such as practicing bully-resistance techniques at home or enrolling the child in a self-defense course.

Finally, do whatever you can to help targets find reasons to feel good about themselves and confident of their ability to deal with bullies in a peaceful manner. Remember, however, that true self-esteem is always earned. Simply telling a child that he is unique and special isn't enough. Children learn to feel good about themselves by recognizing and appreciating their own accomplishments, and by having those accomplishments recognized by others. Accomplishments can take many forms — good deeds, desirable habits, academic success and creative endeavors to name a few. Every child has them. The key is to know the child (and help the child know himself) well enough to identify them.

Teaching Bystanders To Be Upstanders

One of the most important things you can do to curb bullying and assist bully targets is to empower students to speak up and stand up to bullies. Most children find direct confrontation of bullies difficult as it takes a lot of assertiveness and self-confidence to confront a bully. Children also report that they often don't know if its really bullying or if the target needs help. Students need to be taught what bullying looks like and simple, specific actions they would feel comfortable taking when witnessing bully behavior in any form.

Tap into the natural kindness and empathy of students by letting them know that supporting the target is one of the most valuable ways to let targets know they are not alone and that others care about what is happening to them. Teach and encourage all students to reach out in person, or online if appropriate, with messages of support and concern. Targets can be invited to join other kids in activities, at lunch and on the bus or walking home.

Directly teach active listening and inform students that simply listening to others, especially bully targets, is an immensely supportive and healing action that can be taken by anyone at any time.

Let students know that taking action by not participating sends a powerful message that bullying isn't acceptable. A simple statement like, "That's not right." or "Leave him alone." can go a long way toward diffusing an incident. If one child speaks up it can give others the courage to do the same.

Inform students who witness bullying online that they can explicitly not get involved and leave the group. They should take a screen shot of a bully conversation and report it to an adult. They can also react to bullying online by responding with respectful messages or creating their own inclusive, positive and supportive messages.

Teach all students the necessity to tell a trusted adult about any bully incident, and that telling an adult is not tattling but is about helping someone; not about getting someone in trouble. Most importantly, approachable adults and consistent follow through is key to creating an environment where students feel safe in reporting bullying.

How To Change Bully Behavior

Kids who bully need help in understanding the impact their actions have on the target and others. Instruct that bullying is always unacceptable while also helping bullies learn empathy and social skills. Bullies need help in developing problem-solving skills that don't involve aggression. Let them know you believe that they can change their behaviors and develop positive ways of relating to others.

Recognize and reinforce respectful and cooperative behavior whenever it happens. Having students participate in activities where they share feelings and experiences (such as in Sharing Circles) goes a long way in developing empathy and positive ways of interacting in all students.

School wide instruction in social and emotional learning will help bullies develop awareness and learn the necessary skills to change their bully behaviors.

20

How to Use the Activities

There are twenty group activities and twenty-five Sharing Circles in this book. Although the activities and Sharing Circles appear in two different sections, it's recommended that the Sharing Circles be interspersed among the activities choosing the topics that seem most appropriate for supporting or reinforcing each lesson.

- <u>The Group Activities</u> are arranged sequentially and should generally be implemented in the order they appear. The first few activities are devoted to helping children develop a greater awareness of the ingredients and dynamics of bullying — the feelings and reactions it generates in targets and bystanders and the possible motivations of bullies.

  Next, students are given an opportunity to examine their individual rights, to understand how bullying violates those rights, and to recognize the importance of protecting and preserving them.

  Additional activities deal with the importance of reporting bullying incidents. Students identify sources of help and learn how to ask for help. They also plan specific strategies for avoiding bully encounters.

  Students then examine how self-talk affects their vulnerability to bully attacks, and practice using positive self-talk and affirmations to strengthen their resolve in dealing with bullies. They learn relaxation strategies for easing anger and tension, and review specific anger-management strategies.

  Two simple formulas are presented to help students respond quickly and effectively in the heat of a bully encounter. The students are given repeated opportunities to practice these response patterns. Students are also taught how to help targets by becoming upstanders and not just bystanders.

Finally, students identify behaviors that strengthen and erode friendships, and discuss ways of improving their friendship skills.

- Experience Sheets. Most of the group activities in this book include one or more handouts to duplicate and distribute to your students. These "Experience Sheets" direct the students through a variety of exercises — questions to answer, stories to write, pictures to draw, issues to think about. Instructions for incorporating the Experience Sheets are included in the activity outlines. The majority of the sheets are designed to be completed by all participating students in the course of the activity. A few are intended for use in one-to-one sessions with individual targets.

- Sharing Circles. Teaching with group discussion has many benefits. In addition to helping develop a range of skills, it's a powerful and easy way to get students involved. Discussion requires active participation. By exploring different perspectives, experiences and feelings in response to the topic it enhances understanding, cooperation and connections among students. The Sharing Circle rules require members to be respectful and engage in attentive listening which increase peer connections and positive relationships. Talking and interacting positively develops feelings of empathy among all students. Having students participate in regular discussions lays a firm foundation for bully prevention efforts.

In leading the activities and Sharing Circles we urge you to make whatever adjustments are necessary to ensure that each experience is relevant to the ages, abilities, specific needs and cultural mix of your students. For example, some students may require extra help understanding the printed directions on the Experience Sheets. If dyad activities or role plays are new to your students, you may need to model these processes one or more times before asking the students to do them on their own. Or, without using names, you may wish to describe and discuss actual bully encounters that have occurred at your school

How to Lead a Sharing Circle

The Sharing Circle is a structured communication process that provides students a safe place for learning about life and developing important aspects of social-emotional learning. Specifically, the Sharing Circles in this book help students discuss topics related to bullying.

First, we'll provide a brief overview of the process of leading a Sharing Circle and then we'll cover each step in more detail.

A Sharing Circle begins when a group of students and the adult leader sit down together in a circle so that each person is able to see the others easily. The leader of the Sharing Circle briefly greets and welcomes each individual, conveying a feeling of enthusiasm blended with seriousness.

When everyone appears comfortable, the leader takes a few moments to review the Sharing Circle Rules. These rules inform the students of the positive behaviors required of them and guarantees the emotional safety and security, and equality of each member.

After the students understand and agree to follow the rules, the leader announces the topic for the session. A brief elaboration of the topic follows in which the leader provides examples and possibly mentions the topics relationship to prior topics or to other things the students are involved in. Then the leader re-states the topic and allows a little silence during which circle members may review and ponder their own related memories and mentally prepare their verbal response to the topic. (The topics and suggested elaborations are provided with each Sharing Circle in this book..)

Next, the leader invites the circle participants to voluntarily share their responses to the topic, one at a time. No one is forced to share, but everyone is given an opportunity to share while all the other circle members listen attentively. The circle participants tell the group about themselves, their personal experiences, thoughts, feelings, hopes and dreams as they relate to the topic. Most of the circle time is devoted to this sharing phase because of its central importance.

During this time, the leader assumes a dual role—that of leader and participant. The leader makes sure that everyone who wishes to speak is given the opportunity while simultaneously enforcing the rules as necessary. The leader also takes a turn to speak if he or she wishes.

After everyone who wants to share has done so, the leader introduces the next phase of the Sharing Circle by asking several discussion questions. This phase represents a transition to the reflective mode and allows participants to reflect on and express learnings gained from the sharing phase and encourages participants to combine cognitive abilities and emotional experiencing. It's in this phase that participants are able to crystallize learnings and to understand the relevance of the discussion to their daily lives. (Discussion questions for each topic are provided in this book.)

When the students have finished discussing their responses to the questions and the session has reached a natural closure, the leader ends the session. The leader thanks the students for being part of the Sharing Circle and states that it is over.

What follows is a more detailed look at the process of leading a Sharing Circle.

Steps for Leading a Sharing Circle

1. Welcome Sharing Circle members
2. Review the Sharing Circle rules *
3. Introduce the topic
4. Sharing by circle members
5. Ask discussion questions
6. Close the circle

*optional after the first few sessions

1. Welcome Sharing Circle members

   As you sit down with the students in a Sharing Circle group, remember that you are not teaching a lesson. You are facilitating a group of people. Establish a positive atmosphere. In a relaxed manner, address each student by name, using eye contact and conveying warmth. An attitude of seriousness blended with enthusiasm will let the students know that this Sharing Circle group is an important learning experience—an activity that can be interesting and meaningful.

2. Review the Sharing Circle rules

   At the beginning of the first Sharing Circle, and at appropriate intervals thereafter, go over the rules for the circle. They are:

   > **Sharing Circle Rules**
   >
   > ❋ Everyone gets a turn to share, including the leader.
   > ❋ You can skip your turn if you wish.
   > ❋ Listen to the person who is sharing.
   > ❋ There are no interruptions, probing, put-downs, or gossip.
   > ❋ Share the time equally.

   From this point on, demonstrate to the students that you expect them to remember and abide by the ground rules. Convey that you think well of them and know they are fully capable of responsible behavior. Let them know that by coming to the Sharing Circle they are making a commitment to listen and show acceptance and respect for the other students and you. It is helpful to write the rules on chart paper and keep them on display for the benefit of each Sharing Circle session.

3. Introduce the topic

   State the topic, and then in your own words, elaborate and provide examples as each lesson in this book suggests. The introduction or elaboration of the topic is designed to get students focused and thinking about how they will respond to the topic. By providing more than just the mere statement of the topic, the elaboration gives students a few moments to expand their thinking and to make a personal connection to the topic at hand. Add clarifying statements of your own that will help the students understand the topic. Answer questions about the topic, and emphasize that there are no "right" responses. Finally, restate the topic, opening the session to responses (theirs and yours). Sometimes taking your turn first helps the students understand the aim of the topic. The introductions, as written in this book, are provided to give you some general ideas for opening the Sharing Circle. It's important that you adjust and modify the introduction and elaboration to suit the ages, abilities, levels, cultural/ethnic backgrounds and interests of your students.

4. Sharing by circle members

The most important point to remember is this: The purpose of these Sharing Circles is to give students an opportunity to express themselves and *be accepted* for the experiences, thoughts, and feelings they share. Avoid taking the action away from the students. They are the stars!

5. Ask discussion questions

Responding to discussion questions is the cognitive portion of the process. During this phase, the leader asks thought-provoking questions to stimulate free discussion and higher-level thinking. Each Sharing Circle lesson in this book concludes with several discussion questions. At times, you may want to formulate questions that are more appropriate to the level of understanding in your students—or to what was actually shared in the circle. If you wish to make specific connections between the discussion topic and the issue of bullying than you feel is provided by the Discussion Questions provided, ask your own questions that will accomplish that objective.

6. Close the circle

The ideal time to end a Sharing Circle is when the discussion question phase reaches natural closure. Sincerely thank everyone for being part of the circle. Don't thank specific students for speaking, as doing so might convey the impression that speaking is more appreciated than mere listening. Then close the group by saying, "This Sharing Circle is over," or "OK, that ends our circle."

Sharing Circle Rules

❄ Everyone gets a turn to share, including the leader.

❄ You can skip your turn if you wish.

❄ Listen to the person who is sharing.

❄ There are no interruptions, probing, put-downs, or gossip.

❄ Share the time equally.

28

Activities
and
Experience Sheets

30

What Is Bully Behavior?

Purpose:
This activity is designed to help students define, describe and understand bully behavior. It provides an opportunity for students to feel safe in sharing experiences they have had, and to learn that they are not alone in experiencing bully encounters.

Materials:
Experience Sheet, "Bullying Hurts"
Experience Sheet, "Let Off Some Steam"

Procedure:
Ask the students to help you brainstorm a list of typical bully behaviors. Write them on the board. Add the following if they are not suggested by the group:
- demanding money or other objects
- hitting
- making fun of
- name-calling
- damaging personal belongings
- stealing
- laughing at
- yelling at
- excluding (leaving out of activities or groups)
- forcing to do something
- gossiping and telling lies about

Go back over the list and ask for a show of hands from students who have been hit, made fun of, laughed at, called names, etc. Point out that all of these hurtful experiences are the result of bullying.

Distribute the Experience Sheet, "Bullying Hurts," and go over the directions. Allow time for the students to complete the sheet.

> ### What you can do for targets:
> Connect with targets, allowing them to share their experiences and vent their feelings. More than anything else, targets need to feel safe and secure, so address the fear first. Let targets know that you are there to help put an end to the bullying. They don't have to face it alone. Being bullied is not their fault.

When the students have finished writing their stories, ask volunteers to tell (or read) their stories to the group. Remind them to talk about what happened and how they felt, but not to use names. Break the ice by sharing a personal story of your own related to bullying.

Facilitate discussion following each story. Stress that it is important for students to come forward if they are bullied, or witness someone else being bullied. Let the students know that bullying will not be tolerated; however, before bullying can be stopped, incidents of bullying must be reported. Assure them that you will respect their need to remain anonymous.

Explain that you will be helping the students to develop strategies and actions for dealing with bullies, both today and in future sessions.

Give a copy of the Experience Sheet, "Let Off Some Steam" to any student who has actually experienced bullying. Go over the directions. Suggest that these students wait until a time when they can be alone and undisturbed to write their letter. Tell them to be as open as possible about their anger, hurt, humiliation or frustration, telling the bully exactly what they think of him/her. Stress, however, that the letter must not be delivered.

Discussion Questions
1. How do you feel when you see someone acting like a bully? What do you usually do?
2. What have you done to stop bullying behavior?
3. If you haven't done anything, what is stopping you?
4. Why is it important to let bullies know that their behavior is unacceptable?

Bullying Hurts

In the space below, write about one of the following:

- A time you were bullied,
- A time you saw someone else being bullied, or
- A time you bullied another person.

Please don't use any names. Just tell what happened and how you felt.

Let Off Some Steam

Is there a bully in your life? Write a letter to the bully and let him (or her) know exactly how you feel about what is happening.

By putting your feelings down on paper, you can "let off some steam." Write anything you want to say. You are not going to deliver this letter.

When you are finished, keep the letter or throw it away. It's up to you.

Dear Bully,

Now write about some positive and peaceful ways that you might get the bully to leave you alone.

Bullies, Targets, Bystanders, and Upstanders

Purpose:
This activity helps students to define and understand the roles of bully, target and bystander, as well as needs and feelings associated with each role, and to begin developing awareness of how these roles contribute to the bullying problem.

Materials:
Experience Sheet: "A Pound of Cheese for April"
Experience Sheet: "Bullies, Targets, Bystanders, and Upstanders—What Are They Feeling?"

Procedure:
Read "A Pound of Cheese for April." After reading the story, have the students help you define the terms bully, target, bystander, and upstander.

Ask the students:
— Who are the bullies? (April, Lisa and Beth).
— Who is the target? (Jennifer)
— Who are the bystanders? (Jeff, Robbie, Jean, and other kids)
— Who is the upstander (Maria)

Discuss the roles and actions of each character in the story and, without using names, compare to real life examples in the lives of the children. (Comparisons can be made to the stories the children wrote in the previous activity.) Examine the thoughts, feelings and behaviors described in each example.

Make the following points:
- Bullies may look powerful and feel powerful, but down deep they sometimes feel lonely and insecure.
- Bullies usually don't have many friends.
- Targets often lack confidence, feel scared and don't know how to help themselves.

- Targets may not have many (or any) friends to help them.
- Bystanders usually don't know what to do, where to go or how to get help.
- Bystanders may not recognize that bullying is a serious matter, or they may lack the courage to do anything about it.
- Upstanders take action to help the target.

Ask these and other questions to facilitate discussion:
In the story...
1. Did you notice any similarities in the feelings of the bully, the target, the bystanders, or the upstander?
2. What was the body language of a bully? ...of a target?
3. How do you think bystanders feel who do nothing to help a target?
4. How do upstanders feel if they come to the aid of a target?
5. What did Maria do to show her concern for Jennifer?
6. What were some of the ways that Jennifer coped with the experience of being bullied? How well did each of those coping strategies work?
7. How did Jennifer's feelings at the end of the day when she wrote her poem, "April's Last Day at School," differ from her feelings in the morning?

Distribute the Experience Sheet, "Bullies, Targets, Bystanders, and Upstanders" (two pages), and go over the directions. Explain any of the feeling words that the students don't understand, offering examples. Give the students a few minutes to complete the sheet. Afterwards, ask volunteers to share the feelings they listed for each of the roles: target, bully, bystander, and upstander. Facilitate further discussion. Urge the students to take their experience sheets home and talk about bullying with their parents.

A Pound of Cheese for April
By Dianne Schilling and Marika Schilling

Jennifer couldn't see the girls yet, but she could hear them. They were in the same place every morning, under the big elm tree across from the school soccer field. April, Lisa and Beth. Jennifer didn't know the names of very many kids at her new school, and fervently wished that she didn't know these three. Especially April.

"Here comes potato face," April called loudly. She was always the one who started it. The other two snickered and laughed.

Jennifer stared at the sidewalk and kept walking.

"Potato Face isn't talking today," April taunted. "Oh, that's right, I almost forgot. Potatoes are all eyes and no mouth."

Jennifer could hear them behind her, but she didn't turn around. Adjusting her backpack, she hunched forward and tried to make her short, round body look smaller. Yeah, she probably did look like a potato.

"How do you like your potatoes, girls, fried, baked or mashed?" April jeered. "Mashed, don't you think?"

"Yea, mashed," Beth and Lisa parroted in unison.

Jennifer felt her backpack jerk and lost her footing as one of the girls grabbed her from behind and turned her full circle before letting go. Jennifer sat in a heap on the sidewalk while April, Lisa and Beth ran off laughing. They didn't go far.

"Look everybody," April called out to the other kids heading for the school. She pointed to Jennifer. "Look at the mashed potato." Lisa and Beth were doubled over laughing.

Jennifer adjusted her glasses, brushed off her pants and slowly got to her feet. She glanced up at several students who stopped to stare. Two boys from her English class, Jeff and Robbie, were there. They backed away, looking embarrassed. Jean from math class looked at Jennifer sympathetically and shrugged her shoulders, saying nothing.

Jennifer felt a hand on her shoulder and looked around. It was Maria, the only real friend she'd made since transferring to the school three months ago.

"Are you OK, Jen?" asked Maria. "Did you hurt yourself?"

"Hurt myself?" asked Jennifer bitterly. "Do you really think I did this to myself? Didn't you see them knock me down?"

"No," Maria said apologetically. "I just saw you sitting here with everyone laughing."

Jennifer started to cry. "I don't know why they hate me so much," she sobbed. "I haven't done anything to them. I wish I could go back to my old school."

Maria put an arm around Jennifer's shoulders. "Nobody really likes April," she said. "I've known her ever since first grade. She thinks she's a big shot."

"What about Beth and Lisa?" asked Jennifer. "The three of them are always together."

"April bosses them around and they do everything she says. They all live in the same apartment building," Maria explained. "It's kind of run down. I don't think the people who live there are very well off. April invited me over once in the third grade. It was no fun.

Her mother was really mean to her while I was there, so I never went back."

All day long, Jennifer felt miserable. In English class, she scrunched down at her desk and tried not to look at anyone, especially Jeff and Robbie. She was sure the whole school was talking about her. The teacher read some silly poems to the class and talked about creative writing. The homework assignment was to write something funny or crazy. "Make it up or describe something that happened to you," the teacher said. Jennifer doubted that she could find anything funny to write about.

After school, Maria walked Jennifer part way home. When they parted Maria suggested, "Why don't I meet you here on this corner tomorrow morning. We can go the rest of the way to school together. Maybe if I'm with you, April will leave you alone."

Jennifer felt relieved. At least she had one friend. Tomorrow things might be better.

That evening, while finishing her homework, Jennifer thought about the things Maria had said. She wondered if April's mean mother was yelling at her this very minute.

Jennifer missed her old school and the home where she'd grown up, but she was glad to be living in a nice house in a pretty neighborhood. And she felt especially lucky to have nice parents.

For a minute Jennifer almost felt sorry for April. Then she realized that nothing had really changed. April still hated her and would probably call her a bunch of awful names tomorrow, just like she always did. Jennifer smiled.

It was time to write something crazy for English class.

April's Last Day at School

Tuesday at school was very nice;
But a girl named April paid the price,
When at lunch she caused a noisy riot,
Spoiling everyone's noontime diet.

What did April do?
She threw...

A rotten hot dog, a can of hash,
A baloney sandwich from the trash,
Drippy jam, mushy peas
And last but not least, a pound of cheese

Just then, the vice principal came running in.
"Young Lady!" he shouted through the din,
"You shall clean up the mess you've made,
I will make you work like a slave!"

April was never heard from again.
She worked on her knees for days and then
Her mom put her in a sanatorium,
At least that's what they say.

And all because she threw...

A rotten hot dog, a can of hash,
A baloney sandwich from the trash,
Drippy jam, mushy peas
And last but not least, a pound of cheese.

Adapted from a poem by Marika Schilling written when she was 11 years old and being harassed by a bully.

Bullies, Targets, Bystanders, and Upstanders
Everybody Has Feelings

From the list of feeling words on this page, choose as many words as you can to describe how you think each person would feel in a bully encounter. Write the words inside the feet on the next page.

afraid	fearful	outraged
annoyed	foolish	overwhelmed
anxious	frantic	panicked
appreciated	friendly	paranoid
awkward	friendless	persecuted
betrayed	frightened	petrified
bold	helpful	quarrelsome
brave	helpless	sad
caring	hopeless	scared
concerned	horrible	shy
confident	hostile	supportive
cowardly	immobilized	threatened
dejected	impatient	thwarted
desperate	inadequate	trapped
different	infuriated	troubled
disappointed	insecure	uncertain
distraught	intimidated	uneasy
disturbed	isolated	unsettled
embarrassed	lonely	uptight
excited	miserable	vulnerable
exhausted	misunderstood	worried
	nervous	

Bullies, Targets, Bystanders, and Upstanders— What Are They Feeling?

Why Do Bullies Bully?

Purpose:
Students need to understand that bullies are not the tough, self-assured people they appear to be, that they have fears and insecurities of their own. Understanding this reality will give targets a little more courage in facing up to and dealing with bullies and bystanders the courage to become upstanders. This awareness may lead to empathy for the bully, which is okay, but it should not be allowed to produce further tolerance for the bully's behavior.

Materials:
Experience Sheet, "The Bully Mask"

Procedure:
Ask the students to help you brainstorm a list of reasons why bullies do what they do. Accept all contributions and jot them on the board. You will probably hear things like, "They think they're tough," "They like to boss people around," and "They think they're better than everybody else." All of these contributions are valid, and describe how bullies are often perceived by their peers.

Your job is to help the students recognize underlying causes of bullying that might not be apparent to them. Add these to the list. Points that should be made include:

- Bullies lack friends and other healthy support.
- Bullies are often fearful and angry.
- Some bullies are themselves being bullied.
- Bullies may not have love and support at home.
- Bullies usually have learned poor ways of relating to others and don't know how to change their behavior.
- Bullies lack empathy for their targets and other people.

Provide examples wherever possible. To prompt thinking on the part of the students, you may want to refer back to the stories written about bullies in the first activity. Ask the students to try to understand what motivated the bully in their story.

Distribute the experience sheet and allow time for the students to complete it. Then facilitate additional discussion by asking these and other questions:
1. What are bullies usually trying to do to their target?
2. How do bullies usually feel deep inside?
3. Are most bullies well liked and popular? Why or why not?
4. Are bullies brave? Why or why not?
5. Do bullies have high self-esteem? Why or why not?
6. Do bullies pick on strong, self-confident kids? Why or why not?

The Bully Mask

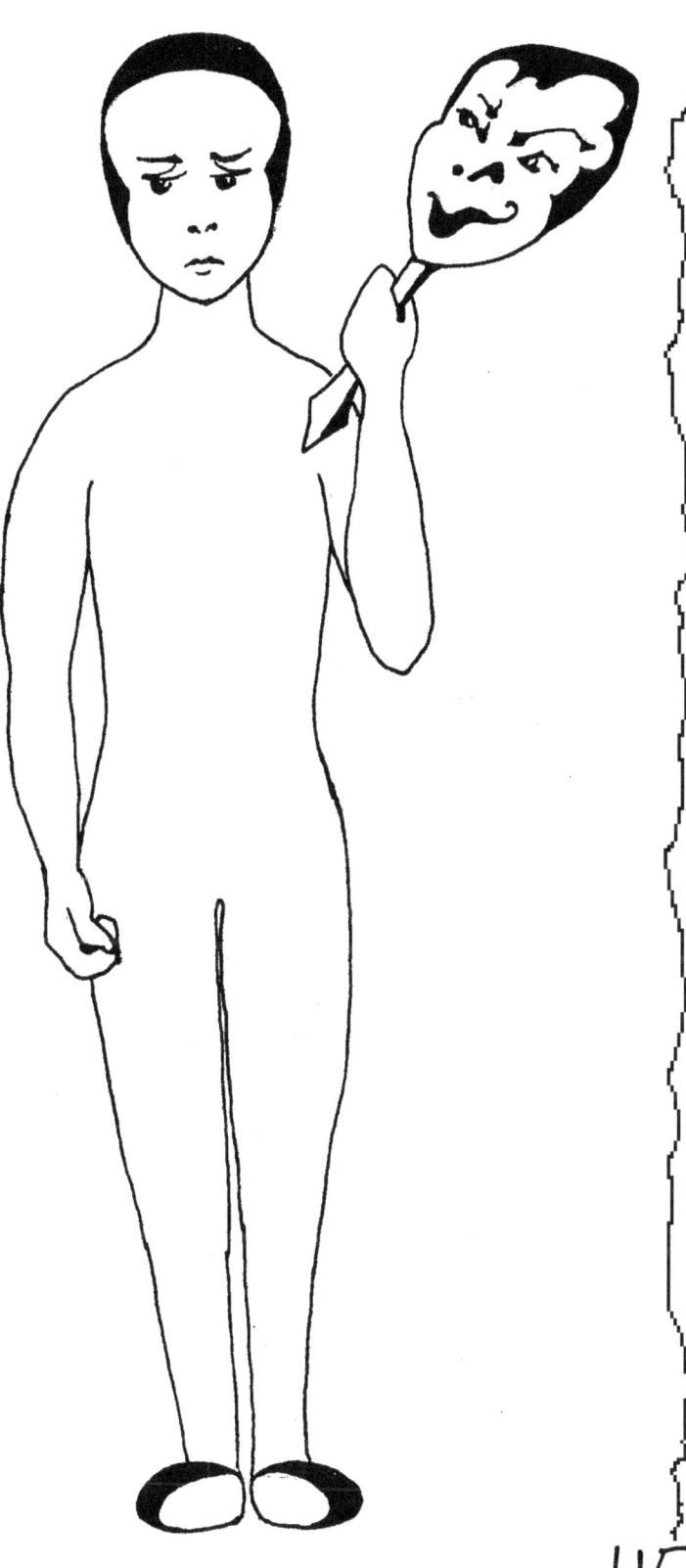

Who is the real person behind the bully mask? Bullies try to appear big, tough and mean. They push kids around as a way of dealing with their own feelings of fear, hurt or anger. They think that by intimidating others, they will feel better about themselves.

Think of a bully you know. If you could rip away the bully's mask, what do you think you would find underneath? Inside the body, write words that describe what is going on deep down inside the bully you know. Write as many words as you can.

Asking for Help

Purpose:
This activity enumerates ten "rights" that all students possess. One of those rights is the right to ask for help. In addition to understanding these rights, students identify resource people and organizations from whom to seek help.

Materials:
Experience Sheet, "Kids Bill of Rights"
Experience Sheet, "A Bully in Your Life? It's Okay to Ask for Help!"

Procedure:
Distribute the Experience Sheet, "Kids Bill of Rights." Ask volunteers to read each of the "rights." As you go through the list, discuss the meaning of each right, using the questions provided (and others, as appropriate).

Discussion Questions:
1. What does the word dignity mean? Why is it important to promote your own dignity?
2. How can you tell when someone respects you?
3. What kinds of actions are disrespectful?
4. Why do we sometimes feel guilty after saying "no" to another person?
5. What can you do when you want to be left alone but someone keeps trying to intrude upon your space?
6. Why do we sometimes change our minds after deciding something?
7. Why is it important to ask for what you want?
8. What can happen if you need help with something, but don't ask for it?
9. What can happen if you need information, like directions, and don't ask for it?
10. Why is it important to feel safe and secure?

Relate the bill of rights to the subject of bullying. Stress that the students have a right to feel safe. When they are targets of a bully, their personal rights are being abused. Also point out that if they are being bullied, it is not their fault and they don't have to face it on their own.

Distribute the Experience Sheet, "A Bully in Your Life? It's Okay to Ask for Help!" Go over the directions and assist the students to fill in the names of various helpers. Stress that resource people and organizations are available within the school and community. Make sure the students know who and what those resources are and where they are located. Check the appropriateness of names they list on their own.

Conclude the activity by discussing when and how to ask for help. Use the discussion questions below, and other appropriate questions. Encourage the students to practice the actual words they would say when asking for help.

Discussion Questions:

1. If you were on your way to school and a bully forced you to hand over your skate board, or jacket, or lunch, to whom would you go for help? When should you go?
2. If a bully kept pressuring you to do something wrong or illegal, how and to whom would you report it? What would you say?
3. If a group of kids were making your life miserable with insults, taunts, and teasing, and you decided to ask me for help, how would you explain the situation to me?
4. If you saw a bully beating up on another student, when and how would you take action? What would you say?
5. If you are the target of online bullying, what should you do? Who can you go to to report the bullying?

Kids Bill of Rights

I have:

1. The right to act in ways that promote my dignity and self-respect as long as the rights of others are not violated in the process.

2. The right to be treated with respect.

3. The right to say "no" and not feel guilty.

4. The right to experience and express my feelings.

5. The right to my own physical and mental space.

6. The right to change my mind.

7. The right to ask for what I want.

8. The right to ask for help if and when I need it.

9. The right to ask for information.

10. The right to be safe and secure.

A Bully in Your Life?
It's Okay to Ask for Help!

If a bully is bothering you, it is important to remember that you don't have to put up with it. And you don't have to handle the problem alone. People are willing to help you, but first they have to know about the problem.

You probably have asked for help with lots of things in your life. On the lines below, write the names of people you would ask for help with...

...homework: _____

...reaching something on a high shelf: _____

...a ride to the movies: _____

...fixing a bike: _____

...finding something on the Internet: _____

If you are being bullied, whom can you tell? Write the names of everyone you can think of.

- _____
- _____
- _____
- _____
- _____
- _____

Now, if you need to, ask for HELP!

Speaking Out Against Bullying

Purpose:
Students who witness bullying may be unsure about what to do and whether to tell someone. This activity mobilizes students who are neither bully nor target to take action.

Materials:
Experience Sheet, "Dealing with Bullies Is Everyone's Responsibility"

Procedure:
Point out that bullying incidents that happen at school can occur in busy places, like hallways, lunch areas, in front of the school and on playgrounds. Although adults don't usually see these incidents, very often other kids are nearby and do witness these incidents, but don't know what to do.

Ask the students to help you brainstorm things that witnesses can do to stop bullies. Add the following ideas if they are not mentioned by the group.
1. Refuse to watch a bullying incident. Bullies want an audience. Never clap or laugh, or boo which can encourage a bully.
2. If appropriate and safe, distract the bully and/or target.
3. Create safety in numbers. If you know that someone is being bullied, make sure that the target is not alone in places where he or she is vulnerable.
4. Support the target by reaching out and letting him or her know you care.
5. Report bullying incidents.

Stress that reporting the incident is very important. Even if the students try other strategies to stop the bully, they should always tell a responsible adult what happened.

Write the following headings on the board:

Who   How

Stress that students should talk to an adult about every bullying incident that occurs. Under "Who," list appropriate adults.

> If you want to ensure that students report the next bullying incident that occurs, you must show them that you (and other adults) will take action. The students must see that telling is relevant and rewarding and ideas that they put forth are honored and implemented.

Discuss ways of reporting that guard the safety of students, such as writing an anonymous note, going to the office after school when the rest of the kids have gone home, or calling a teacher/counselor from home. List these ideas under "How." Make a distinction between tattling or snitching and reporting an incident. Tattling is about wanting to get someone in trouble. Informing an adult is about wanting to help a target.

Distribute the experience sheet and go over the directions. After allowing the students time to complete the sheet, ask volunteers to read their top five ideas. Facilitate discussion. Try to honor and implement ideas that seem workable, developing actions plans, as needed.

Dealing With Bullies Is Everyone's Responsibility

It is up to everyone in the school to stop hurtful and teasing behavior. When you and other kids decide that it is time to stand up to a bully, to be an upstander not just a bystander, you can really make a difference. When you mobilize and take action, you can help put an end to bully behavior. Wouldn't you like to have a school with no bullies? What can be done to stop bullies from harassing others? List your ideas here:

- _____
- _____
- _____
- _____
- _____
- _____

What can you do to stop bullies?

- _____
- _____
- _____
- _____
- _____
- _____

Cross out any ideas that involve violence or retaliation. When you use violence against a bully, you are doing the same thing you want him (or her) to stop doing. Besides, violence usually makes things worse.

Go back and look at each of your ideas. Ask yourself, "Will this idea really work to stop a bully?" Put an X beside any idea that probably will not work.

Now, pick your five best ideas and number them #1 to #5. Make your very best idea #1. That's the idea you should try first!

How to Avoid a Bully

Purpose:
In this activity, students identify areas of the school and community where bullying is likely to take place, describe the reasons each location is conducive to bullying, and identify appropriate avoidance tactics for keeping away from a bully.

Materials:
Experience Sheet, "How to Avoid a Bully"
Experience Sheet, "A New Route to School"

Procedure:
Ask the students where they have seen bullying incidents take place. Caution them not to use names, just to briefly describe what happened and where. Solicit specific locations in the school building, on the school grounds and in the community. List these locations on the board and facilitate discussion. Ask:
- What do these places have in common? (remote, no adults, etc.).
- How are these locations different from places where kids don't usually get bullied? (lots of people, visible to adults, etc.)

Ask the students to help you brainstorm ways for kids to avoid a bully. List their ideas on the board. Include the following methods if they are not mentioned by the students:
- Take a different route to school.
- Stay in places where there are other people.
- Stay close to adults.
- Don't go off alone.
- Hang out with a large group of people.

Distribute the Experience Sheet, "How to Avoid a Bully." Direct the students to complete the sheet using suggestions from the board and anything else they can think of.

When the students have completed the experience sheet, continue the discussion. Encourage the students to offer ideas and solutions and to share their own experiences. Discuss various outcomes that could result from their ideas.

What you can do for targets:

If you are working with a student who is being bullied on the way to or from school, give that student the experience sheet, "A New Route to School." Work with the student to create the map. Discuss this new route, its relative safety, and the wisdom of using it.

Discussion Questions:

1. Why do bullies like to catch their targets alone?
2. When bullies tease or harass a target in front of other kids, what are they trying to get (or prove)?
3. Why is it better to outsmart bullies than to outfight or out tease them?
4. How do you feel about yourself when you outsmart a bully?

How to Avoid a Bully

If you have ever been bullied, or seen someone else being bullied, think about the places where bullying takes place. List those places in the left-hand column. Across from each bullying location, in the right-hand column, describe a way to avoid being bullied in that particular place.

Where Bullying Takes Place	How to Avoid Being Bullied

A New Route to School

Sometimes the best choice you can make is to avoid a bully. If someone always picks on you in about the same place on your way to or from school, find another route. In the space below, use a pencil to draw a street map of your normal route to and from school. Then take a pen and draw a new, safe route that you can begin using.

Are there safe spots on your new route?
Are adults or other kids around who can help if the bully shows up? Mark these "safe spots" on your map. Remember, there is safety in numbers.

List the names of kids you can walk with:

- _____
- _____
- _____
- _____
- _____
- _____

New-Kid Welcome Kits

Purpose:
Children who are new to a school with no friends or support groups can easily become targets for a bully. A Welcome Kit can help to make the new kid feel more comfortable and secure. It can also serve as an introduction to new friends and connections in the school.

Materials:
multiple copies of an appropriate organizer, e.g., inexpensive 3-ring binders, expandable file folders, large envelopes, presentation folders with pockets, etc.; art materials

Procedure:
Begin this activity by asking the students: "What is it like to be a new kid at school? How many of you have had that experience?"

Invite volunteers to share what it's like to enter a new school where you don't know anyone. Ask them if anyone showed them around during the first week or so, and whether or not the staff and students were welcoming and friendly. Point out that one of the nicest things they can do is to make a new student feel a part of the school from the very first day.

Announce that, as a service project, the students are going to prepare "welcome kits" to give to new students.

As a total group, brainstorm the contents of the kit. Try to think of as many things as possible that a new student might find useful or encouraging. Follow the rules of brainstorming, i.e., anything goes, be creative, no evaluation during the brainstorming process, no put downs of any kind. Your list might include:
- a map of the school
- information about the school (description, history, unique characteristics, special relationships, e.g., with local colleges or businesses)
- a school district telephone directory (perhaps an abbreviated version)
- a school calendar, with special events marked
- a student handbook or list of rules/requirements

- information about teachers (names, classes, room numbers)
- information about office staff
- lists of sports, service groups, and clubs, with information on how they are organized and how to become involved
- descriptions of future school events, including dates and times
- location of lost and found
- jokes, cartoons, or stories authored by students
- student-made coupons redeemable for special services, e.g., a campus tour, help with homework, introductions to six kids, a recess game partner, etc.
- a copy of the student newspaper
- PTA information
- a map of the town or city
- names and telephone numbers of local medical facilities
- coupons for treats at local stores and businesses
- information about public transportation
- a candy bar or treat

After the brainstorming process is concluded, go back and evaluate the list, narrow it down and make final selections.

Choose teams of volunteers to obtain or prepare the various items needed. When everything has been collected, appoint an "assembly team" to:
1. Decide on the best presentation of the items.
2. Put together a model kit
3. Design and produce a cover
3. Develop a system for efficiently assembling the kits.

Appoint another team to answer distribution questions. Have them consider the pros and cons of several distribution alternatives. For example:
- Assign a person to hand deliver each kit and perhaps act as a companion/guide throughout the first day.
- Mail the kit.
- Deliver the kit to the home of the new student.
- Give out kits at a monthly "newcomers" reception or party.
- Decide how they will communicate with the school administrators.

When the kits are finished and all of the decisions regarding distribution have been made, facilitate a culminating discussion.

Discussion Questions:
1. How do you feel when you do something to help a person you don't yet know?
2. How would you feel if a friendly student presented you with a kit like this when you entered a new school?
3. How do we benefit from reaching out to others?

What I Like and Respect About Me

Purpose:
Students who have a strong sense of self-worth and self-respect are much less likely to be the target of a bully. This activity helps students identify and focus on their own positive and respectable traits thereby helping to develop self-worth.

Materials:
chart paper and markers; paper and pencils for individual writing

Procedure:
Ask the students to brainstorm qualities, attributes and characteristics of people they respect. List those descriptors on a chart. For example, the chart might look like this:

We respect people who are:
- generous
- willing to share
- concerned about others
- honest
- happy
- sincere

If the students need help listing characteristics, call on volunteers to think of an individual whom they respect and tell about that person.

Next, ask the students to take a piece of paper and write their names at the top and then list three to four things that they like and respect about themselves. Circulate and assist students who need help. Have them refer to the list on the chart to pick characteristics they see in themselves

Place the lists in a container and save them for subsequent sessions.

At a follow-up session, pull one name out of the container. Have the person whose name is on the paper come to the front of the room (or the center of the circle). Do <u>not</u> read the three or four items on the list. In your own words, explain to the group:

"(Juanita) is our 'star,' and we are going to go around the room and take turns guessing what she wrote on her list. When it's your turn to guess, you might ask, '(Juanita), did you write that you like and respect yourself for being a loyal friend?' or '(Juanita), did you write that you like and respect yourself for being honest?' (Juanita) will respond with either, 'Thank you, that is what I wrote down,' or 'Thank you, but that's not it.'"

Keep going around the circle until all three characteristics have been named or until every student has made a guess. If the three characteristics have not been named by the conclusion of the round, have the "star" tell his or her three characteristics to the group.

Repeat this activity throughout the year, making sure that every participant has the chance to be the "star."

Variation:

If you choose to conduct this activity in one or two sessions, break the students into small groups for them to guess what the "star" wrote on her list. Have all the groups go through the process simultaneously while you circulate making sure everyone gets a chance to be the "star". Conclude the activity by asking the Discussion Questions.

In a summary discussion, make these points:
- Identifying our own strengths helps us to feel good about who we are. We become more likable and respectable to ourselves.
- How we feel about ourselves deep down inside is just as important, maybe even more important, than how others feel about us.

Discussion Questions:
1. Why do we like and respect certain traits and not others?
2. Why is it important to know what our strengths are?
3. Are people who respect themselves likely to stand up to bully behavior better than people who don't? Why or why not?

Positive Self-Talk

Purpose:
Self-talk can play a critical role in determining the outcome of a bullying situation. This activity demonstrates the importance of positive self-talk, and prepares students to use positive self-talk in bully encounters.

Materials:
Experience Sheet, "What Do You Say When You Talk to Yourself? Make It Something Nice!"

Procedure:
Write the term *self-talk* on the board and ask the students what it means to them. Facilitate discussion, using language and examples appropriate to the age of the students. Be sure to cover the following points:

- We all have hundreds of conversations with ourselves every day. (Give examples.)
- Self-talk consists of the words that you say about you, either silently to yourself or audibly to another person.
- Everything you say about yourself (your self-talk) enters your subconscious mind.
- The subconscious mind believes anything you tell it, whether true or false. It makes no moral judgments. Like a computer, the subconscious accepts and acts on whatever input you give it. Whatever you put in, you get back.
- When you say things about yourself that are negative, you are directing your subconscious to make you behave like a person with those negative qualities. When you say positive things about yourself, you are directing your subconscious to make you behave in positive ways.
- Self-talk is closely related to personal effectiveness. Positive self-talk adds to your personal effectiveness. Negative self-talk robs you of effectiveness. The more positive self-talk you use, the greater your personal power, and the more control you have over your life.
- Positive self-talk better equips you are to defend yourself in any situation.

Write the headings, "Positive Self-Talk" and Negative Self-Talk" on the board. Ask the students to help you brainstorm a list of statements to write under each heading. Include statements that the students recall making, as well as statements they have heard others make. (Most likely, the negative self-talk list will be longer.)

Ask the students:
- Which self-talk statements are most likely to be running through a person's mind when he or she is being bullied?
- What self-talk statements run through the minds of people who are often the targets of bullying?

Put a check mark beside each identified statement.

Brainstorm positive self-talk statements that can be used instead of the negative statements listed (and checked off). Write these on the board.

Point out that by thinking positive self-talk statements, students are more likely to feel good about themselves and their abilities. The better they feel about themselves, the more equipped they are to defend against bullies.

Distribute the Experience Sheet. Leave all of the brainstormed information on the board for the students to refer to while they complete the sheet. Encourage the students to create a simple phrase to repeat to themselves that will help build their self-confidence.

What you can do for targets:

Brainstorm with targets how they can develop affirming self-talk. Once you have a pretty good idea what a bully's abusive behavior is, help the target create a "mantra" or self-talk phrase that can be repeated when face-to-face with the bully. For example, if the child is being teased and called "fatso," the mantra might be, "I know I'm a likeable, good kid. I feel good about me."

Extension:
Have the students practice the use of positive self-talk in role-plays of bully encounters.

What Do You Say When You Talk to Yourself? Make It Something Nice!

Always remember that you are a special person. You have the right to feel safe and protected. Believe in yourself and have confidence that you can handle bullies in a positive and peaceful manner.

Write some of the negative things you say about yourself in the left-hand column. In the right-hand column, write a positive self-talk statement you can use instead.

Negative Self-Talk	Positive Self-Talk
_____	_____
_____	_____
_____	_____
_____	_____

Now, go back and draw a thick black line through every negative self-talk statement. As you draw each line, repeat to yourself,

"I will never say this to myself again."

Next, circle every positive self-talk statement. As you draw each circle, think to yourself how true the statement is. Promise yourself that, starting now, you will say or think this statement to yourself often.

Creating Positive Affirmations

Purpose:
By deliberately affirming that they do certain things well, students reinforce their strengths and positive attributes. Knowing that targets are inclined to focus on their weaknesses, this activity goes a step further, showing students how to construct positive affirmations around skills, abilities and qualities they would like to cultivate or improve.

Materials:
Experience Sheet, "Affirmations."

Procedure:
Distribute both pages of the experience sheet and go over the directions. On the board, write these guidelines for constructing an affirmation:
- Write the affirmation in the present tense. Say, "I am…" rather than "I will…"
- Be specific. For example, if gymnastics is your focus, specify in which area of gymnastics you are improving, such as parallel bars, rings, freestyle, etc.
- Repeat each affirmation often. Picture yourself exhibiting the attribute or performing the skill perfectly.

What you can do for targets:
Help targets develop positive affirmations that they can use in bully encounters and at other times. Role play the affirmations with the child. Encourage their consistent use.

After the students have completed the experience sheet, have them get together in groups of two or three and practice delivering their affirmations aloud and with conviction. Urge the students to coach and encourage each other. Afterwards, facilitate a brief discussion.

Discussion Questions:
1. How difficult was it to list ten things that you do well?
2. What happens to our self-esteem when we get recognized for doing a good job?
3. Why is it important to give ourselves praise and recognition, even if others don't?
4. What did it feel like to role play your affirmations?

Affirmations

List ten things that you do well. Include anything that you feel good about, small or large, such as reading, dancing, pitching a fast ball, skateboarding, programming a computer, or being a friend.

1. _____
2. _____
3. _____
4. _____
5. _____
6. _____
7. _____
8. _____
9. _____
10. _____

Choose three items from your list and write an affirmation for each one. For example, "I enjoy reading," "I'm a terrific dancer," or "I am a good friend."

1. _____
2. _____
3. _____

Now list five things you would like to do better. For example, maybe you want to improve your ability in math, public speaking, making new friends, or playing a musical instrument.

1. _____
2. _____
3. _____
4. _____
5. _____

Choose two items from the list above and write an affirmation for each one. Write the affirmation as if you already had the skill or ability. For example, "Math comes easily to me," "I am poised and confident when speaking to a group," "I make a new friend every week.," or "I enjoy reading."

1. _____

2. _____

What's Your Style? Aggressive, Passive or Assertive

Purpose:
Since bullies often tune into others' lack of self-confidence, this activity helps students become aware of and practice assertive behaviors.

Materials:
Experience Sheet, "Reacting Assertively"

Procedure:
Write the words, "Passive," "Aggressive," and "Assertive" on the board. Explain to the students that these labels represent styles of responding to people and events. Two of the styles tend to create problems. The third style is usually very effective.

Using the following information, explain the styles, giving an example of each.

Aggressive
An aggressive person acts like a bully and pushes others around—physically, verbally, or both. He or she responds to situations by speaking loudly, acting or sounding angry, using threats, accusations, and name-calling. An aggressive person doesn't respect the rights of others and can make you feel angry, hurt, or scared.

Passive
A passive person is what you might call "wishy-washy." He or she speaks very softly, slumps, doesn't look at you, and may even appear scared or nervous. Passive people feel unsure. They usually let others make the decisions, and then go along with those decisions—even when they are dangerous or wrong. Passive people often get pushed around or bullied.

Assertive
If you usually stand up for what you want, while respecting the rights of others, you probably have an assertive response style. You look directly at others without staring in a threatening

way, and you speak up confidently, without yelling. You don't always do what the crowd does. You follow through on your responsibilities to other people.

Read the situations below, and ask volunteers to demonstrate how a person might respond using each of the three response styles.

1. The class is on the basketball court, and is choosing teams for a game. You want to play center, but so do two other students.

2. You are at a birthday party. The kids start talking about playing a mean trick on a friend of yours who is not there.

3. Two friends come to your house one Saturday and ask if they can come in. Your parents are gone for the day, and told you not to have company. You want to obey your parents, but your friends make it hard for you. They insist that no one will know.

Distribute the three-page experience sheet and go over the instructions. Allow the students time to complete the sheet individually, then ask them to form groups of four or five. Direct the groups to dramatize the three situations described on the experience sheet, taking turns playing the aggressive, passive and assertive roles. Circulate and assist. If time permits, ask some of the groups to repeat their dramatizations for the entire class.

Lead a summary discussion. Ask the students to think about the three response styles and answer these questions.

Discussion Questions:
1. What are the main differences between the response styles?
2. Which response style is the most effective? Why?
3. How can a passive person become more assertive?
4. How can an aggressive person become more assertive?

Extension:

Since role-play is such a powerful means of internalizing new behaviors, an additional role-play option is described here.

Ask the students to form groups of three. Have the members of each group divide the three response roles (aggressive, passive and assertive) between them. Give each group a copy of the response situations described below.

Have the groups role-play each situation three times, with each member of the group responding according to his or her role. Instruct them to switch response roles between situations, so that every member has a chance to practice all three response styles. When it is not their turn to respond to a situation, group members are to play the other roles in the scenario or act as "drama coach," to the responder. Encourage the students to get in touch with their feelings in each role, and to dramatically demonstrate the differences between the three styles.

Response Situations
1. You and your friend plan to go to a movie this weekend, but you can't agree on what movie to see. Your friend picked the movie last time, so you think it's your turn to choose. However, your friend is resisting because his or her parent already saw the movie you've chosen and didn't like it.

2. You are standing in a long cafeteria line, waiting to order your lunch and a drink. Just as your turn comes up, another student cuts in, saying that he or she is in a big hurry and can't wait. When you object, the student first pleads, then starts to get angry, calling you names.

3. You and your brother (or sister) share a room. Your parent has threatened to ground you both for the weekend if the room isn't cleaned up before supper today. You always keep your things neat, and think that your brother should do the cleaning, since it's his mess. Your brother says he won't do anything unless you help.

> ### What you can do for Targets:
>
> Role play with targets so that they have many opportunities to practice assertive skills: standing up straight; looking someone in the eye when speaking; and talking in a positive, steady voice. Brainstorm with targets simple, easy responses that they can use in a real bully encounter. Examples of easily remembered responses are:
> "I don't like what you're doing. Stop it."
> "Go away and leave me alone."
> End each role play with the target standing tall and walking away.

Reacting Assertively

Read these situations and decide which response is aggressive, which is passive, and which is assertive. After each response, circle your choice. When you have finished, get together with your group and act out the situations.

Agressive   Assertive   Passive

Situation I:
You and some friends are having a conversation outside a convenience store after school. A police officer approaches and begins questioning you about your activities.

Responses:
1. You step back, look at the ground, and let one of your friends do all the talking.
  Aggressive Passive Assertive

2. You stand up straight and speak up clearly, answering all of the officer's questions in a straight forward way.
  Aggressive Passive Assertive

3. You roll your eyes at your friends, become defensive, and demand to know what the officer thinks you're doing.
  Aggressive Passive Assertive

Situation II

You and two other students are working as a team on a computer project. You start to argue concerning what step should come next, and in the process raise your voices and begin gesturing and pushing each other around in a friendly way. Your teacher breaks up the argument, sends you to your desks, and tells you that you will have to finish the assignment separately.

Responses:

1. You shrug your shoulders, go to your desk, and spend the rest of the period sullenly doodling in the margin of your book.
   Aggressive   Passive   Assertive

2. You wait until the teacher is finished talking, then state that you would like to explain what happened. You acknowledge that you were loud and may have disrupted the class and promise to be more careful when you have disagreements in the future. You say that, in your opinion, all members of the team will do a better job on the assignment and learn more if allowed to continue working together.
   Aggressive   Passive   Assertive

3. You complain loudly that the teacher isn't being fair because you were only having a normal disagreement. You tell the teacher that if you can't finish the project it won't be your fault, and make a face when he or she turns away.
   Aggressive   Passive   Assertive

Situation III:
A few weeks ago, your parent outlined some chores for you to do around the house and yard on a regular basis. You are getting behind in those chores because of activities at school and with your friends. Your parent threatens to ground you if you don't catch up on your chores within the next couple of days.

Responses:
1. You apologize, explaining that you, too, have been concerned about the chores because of a recent increase in your other activities. You ask your parent to help you work out a schedule that better utilizes your time.

        Aggressive   Passive   Assertive

2. You listen sullenly, then go in your room and cry, all the while telling yourself that your parent is mean and is deliberately making life miserable for you.

        Aggressive   Passive   Assertive

3. You get angry and tell your parent that he or she is being unfair. You go outside, slamming the door behind you, and start banging tools around as you work in the yard.

        Aggressive   Passive   Assertive

Practice being assertive!
Respect the rights of others and stand up for your own.

Developing Listening Skills

Purpose:
This activity introduces important communication concepts, and gives students an opportunity to learn and practice skills associated with active listening. Active listening is a valuable skill to use in supporting the target of a bully.

Materials:
Experience sheet, "Active Listening"

Procedure:
Tell the students that they are going to practice one of the most important communication skills they will ever learn — Active Listening. Write the term on the board, underline the word Active, and ask the students how they think active listening differs from the kind of listening they do all day long, every day.

Accept all ideas and begin to facilitate a discussion about the importance of listening. You might ask the students how they feel when someone really listens to them, and what it feels like to be interrupted or to realize that the other person didn't hear a word they said. In the course of your discussion, make the following points about listening:
- Good listeners are rare.
- In most conversations, people are more concerned with what they want to say than what the other person is saying.
- Good listening requires focus, concentration, and energy.
- To really listen, you have to keep an open mind and heart.
- Listening all by itself is the most effective way to help and support someone who has been the target of a bully

Distribute the "Active Listening" experience sheets. Go over the steps to active listening.

Four Steps to Active Listening
1. Look at the person who is talking.
2. Listen carefully to his or her words.
3. Notice the feelings that go with the words.
4. Say something to show that you have been listening.

Discuss specific behaviors involved in each step. For example, point out that listening to the words requires thinking about and understanding their meaning from the speaker's point of view. Noticing feelings involves paying attention to the speaker's tone of voice, facial expression, and posture, and empathizing — imagining what it would be like to be in the speaker's shoes. Saying something back not only proves that you are listening, it helps the speaker clarify his or her thoughts and allows you to check to make sure you are "getting the message."

Demonstrate with a volunteer. Ask a child to join you in the front of the room and to talk for a couple of minutes about something that is important to him or her. Instruct the students to watch carefully and notice what you do. Allow the demonstration to continue long enough for you to give four or five active listening responses. Then thank the volunteer and ask the observers to describe what they saw. Clarify the process and answer questions.

Have the students form groups of six. Ask each group to choose a topic from the board (topic suggestions are listed at the end of this activity). In your own words, give the groups these instructions:

One person at a time will speak to the topic for 1 minute. When it is your turn, before you speak, you must give an active listening response (restate or paraphrase) what the person before you said. Look at the person when you do this. If you are the first person to speak, you will speak again just to restate the contribution of the last person.

Time the 1-minute intervals and signal when it is time to switch. After every student has had a turn to speak, signal the students to stop. Briefly ask each group how it went, clarifying further, as needed. Then, if time allows, have the groups choose a second topic and repeat the procedure. Conclude the activity with a summary discussion.

Discussion Questions:
1. What was the easiest thing about active listening.
2. What was most difficult?
3. How did it feel to be listened to?
4. Why do people so seldom stop and really listen to each other?
5. How do you think active listening helps people who have been bullied?

Discussion Topics:
- What I'd like to do this weekend
- A skill I'm trying to improve
- Something I'm worried about
- My hardest subject in school
- The best time I ever had with a friend

Active Listening

What is Active Listening? It's when you listen very carefully and try to understand the ideas and feelings of another person from his or her point of view.

Four Steps to Active Listening

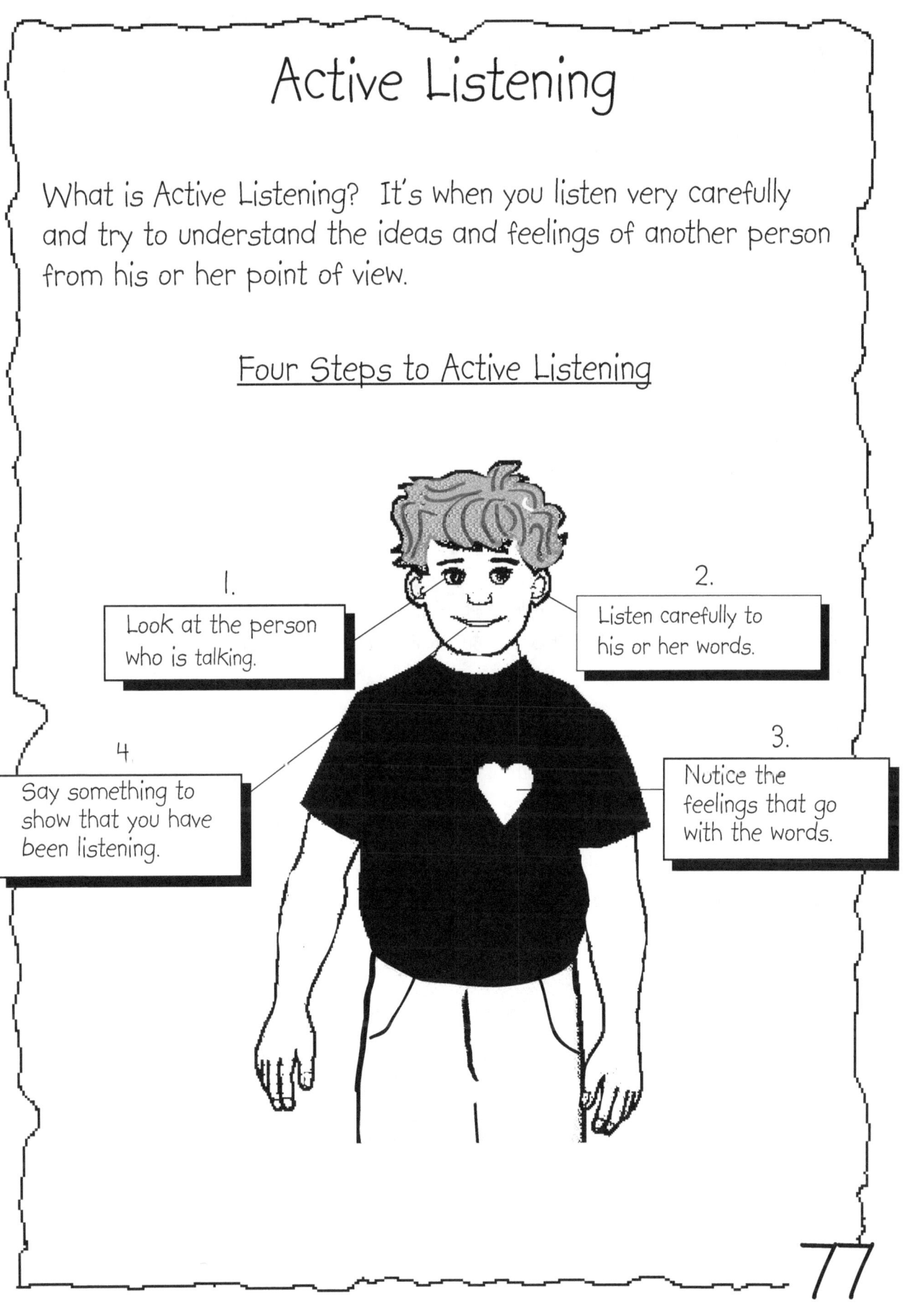

1. Look at the person who is talking.
2. Listen carefully to his or her words.
3. Notice the feelings that go with the words.
4. Say something to show that you have been listening.

Relaxation and Anger Management Strategies

Purpose:
Anger is a normal human emotion, and all students benefit from learning strategies and techniques for controlling anger. Targets and bullies generally carry a great deal of anger inside and are special beneficiaries of anger-management strategies.

Materials:
Experience Sheet, "Expressing Anger"

Procedure:
Begin by discussing with the students the idea that getting angry is normal, and involves reactions that generally come naturally. Ask volunteers to describe times when they felt extremely angry and "blew their top" without thinking about the consequences. Share an example of your own, too.

After several examples, ask the students if they would like to learn some simple, easy-to-remember techniques for managing their anger in healthy and satisfying ways.

Explain that strenuous physical activity is a good way to "work off steam," but when a workout is just not possible, it helps to have alternative techniques. For example, if you get angry in a public place, or in the middle of class, you need quiet ways to control anger.

Tell the students that you are going to teach them four easy ways to control anger quietly: deep breathing, counting, and two techniques called "Hook-ups" and "Positive Points."

Explain and demonstrate one strategy at a time. Have the students practice after each demonstration.

Belly Breathing

Explain that belly breathing is taking in breaths slowly and deeply so that the diaphragm is extended. This is an important point. Children tend to extend their chests and think that they are breathing deeply. However, for a breath to be deep, the air must push down on the diaphragm, which extends the belly.

Give (and demonstrate) these directions:
1. Breathe in deeply and hold the breath for about two seconds.
2. Slowly release the breath, making sure that all of the breath is out.
3. Hold that position for three or more seconds while relaxing the body.
4. Repeat five to ten times.

The students will notice that their breathing becomes slower and more natural as they continue. It is important that they concentrate solely on breathing. Tell them to listen to the air entering the lungs, to hold and hear the exhalation, and to hold before repeating the process. Suggest that they close their eyes and relax their bodies and minds. If they do this when they are angry, much of the angry energy will dissipate.

Counting

Counting is something anyone can do to stay cool in tense or potentially explosive situations. Give (and demonstrate) these directions:
1. Slowly and silently count to ten. (This can also be done aloud, in appropriate situations.)
2. Next, slowly count backwards from ten.
3. Concentrate on counting, nothing more.
4. Repeat the process as many times as necessary until you feel under control.
5. If you want to count to 25, go ahead. The important thing is to think about the numbers you are counting, drawing your attention away from the angry situation.

Hook-ups*

Explain that this body position achieves its calming effect by focusing attention on oneself rather than on the external situation. It can create feelings of safety and peace. At the very least, the concentration required to achieve and hold the position makes staying angry rather difficult.

Give (and demonstrate) these directions:
1. Stand, sit or lie down.
2. Cross one ankle over the other.
3. Hold both arms out straight in front of the body with the backs of the hands facing each other, thumbs pointing toward the floor.
4. Cross one hand over the other and clasp the hands as if shaking hands with yourself.
5. Roll the hands downward and into the body, resting them against the chest.
6. Touch the tip of the tongue against the roof of the mouth. (The tongue position is thought to stimulate a connection between the emotional and reasoning parts of the brain.)
7. Hold this position for as long as it takes to calm down (usually a minute or so but may require more time, depending on the intensity of the anger).

Positive Points*

Ask the students if they have ever noticed someone under stress touch the forehead above the eyebrows and massage that area. Explain that this area of the forehead is thought to house emotional stress-release points.

Give (and demonstrate) these directions:
1. Place the tips of your fingers on the indentations of the forehead a half inch or so above each of the eyebrows.
2. Close your eyes.
3. Hold your hands in place for a few minutes.
4. Notice how you begin to relax and take on a more positive outlook.

Distribute the experience sheet and go over the directions. Give the students time to write their stories. When finished, have the students share their stories in small groups, or invite volunteers to read their stories to the total group. Facilitate discussion.

Discussion Questions:
1. Why is it sometimes so difficult to keep anger from "exploding?"
2. What happens when you explode like that at home? ...at school?
3. What strategy did you use to change your story and manage your angry feelings?
4. How can you remind yourself to use that strategy the next time you get angry?
5. How can learning to manage a strong feeling like anger help you to better manage other strong feelings like sadness or jealousy?

Extension:
1. To anchor these new skills, have the students pair up and take turns teaching each other a strategy.
2. Ask the students to try one or more of these strategies the next time they are angry, and to report back how well the strategy worked.

* Adapted from Brain Gym, Teachers Edition, revised; by Dr. Paul Dennison and Gail Dennison, Edu-Kinesthetics, Inc, Ventura, CA: 1989.

Expressing Anger

Think of a time when you got really, really angry. Something exploded inside of you. Without using any names, describe the event, what you did, and how you felt.

How could you have managed yourself in a better and more positive manner? Create a different ending to the above story, with you using a positive strategy to manage your angry feelings.

Reach for the Sky – Developing Confident Behaviors

Purpose:
When students develop positive attitudes about themselves and learn behaviors that reflect those attitudes, they are likely to develop healthy friendships and not be target to bullying.

Materials:
Experience Sheet, "Reach for the Sky"

Procedure:
Remind the students of the value of positive self-talk and of behaving in a confident, assertive manner. Point out that bullies often gain power because targets don't know how to act, or react. Announce that you are going to teach them a very simple formula that will make them feel more powerful. Once they have learned this formula, they can think it, and use it, whenever they need a shot of self-confidence.

Have the students stand around the edge of the room. Say to them "Stand up as tall as you can and imagine that you are reaching for the sky with the top of your head." Demonstrate this posture.

Ask the students to describe the sensations they experience reaching for the sky with the tops of their heads. You will get a variety of responses. Accept them all.

Tell the students to start walking around the room. As they walk, say to them, "Walk straight and tall with your head held high, like it's touching the sky. Think to yourself, 'I have self-confidence and high self-esteem. I know I'm someone special. I feel good about me.'" Allow enough time for the students to really get into the exercise.

Distribute both pages of the experience sheet, go over the directions, and give the students a few minutes to complete it. When they have finished, ask volunteers to read some of the things they wrote on the inside and the outside of the body to build and demonstrate self-confidence. Facilitate discussion.

Discussion Questions:
1. How do you feel when you walk straight and tall?
2. How do you think a bully would react if, instead of acting afraid, you walked straight and tall?
3. What are some other things that you can do to build self-confidence?
4. Why do bullies avoid self-confident people?

Reach for the Sky

Sometimes kids get picked on because they look like easy targets. Remember, deep down, bullies are really unsure of themselves, so they need to find and pick on someone who doesn't look very confident. If you learn to stand tall, hold your head up, walk with confidence and purpose, and think positive thoughts about yourself, you won't look like a very good target to a bully. Remember to always...

- **Think Tall!**
- **Stand Tall!**
- **Walk Tall!**
- **Believe Tall!**

On the inside of the body, write things that you can think and feel that will give you self-confidence and make you feel good about yourself. On the outside of the body, write things that you can do to show your self-confidence to other people

Reach for the Sky

Say No, Then Go

Purpose:
This activity provides another simple, assertive formula for students to learn and implement when faced with a bully encounter.

Materials:
Experience Sheet, "Say No and Go"

Procedure:
Distribute both pages of the experience sheet and go over the directions. Discuss the cartoon and what the students can learn from it. Talk about the value of remembering two little words, "no" and "go." Explain that, if the students can remember to use these words and walk away with confidence, they will have learned a powerful way to handle bullies.

Give the students time to write their stories.

When they have finished, invite volunteers to read their stories to the group. (If you have a bully story, this would be a good time to share it.)

After several students have shared their stories, select one incident to role play. Ask the author to play him/herself, and choose volunteers to play the bully and any other characters in the story.

Direct the cast to role play the story three times — first with the ending as it actually happened; second, with the new assertive ending written by the author; and third, using the "no" and "go" formula.

> **What you can do for targets:**
> Since role-play actually develops skills (rather than just talking about them), this is an important formula for targets to role-play.

Say No and Go

Do you *see* what is happening in the cartoon? This person is not going to be bullied again. He simply says, "no" loud and clear, and in an assertive manner. Then he walks away. He remembers to stand tall, hold his head up and think good thoughts about himself.

- Think Tall!
  - Stand Tall!
    - Walk Tall!
      - Believe Tall!

In your mind, *see* yourself doing these things. Visualize and practice in your head often. The next time you are face to face with a bully, you will know what to do.

Just say no and go.

In the space below, write a story about a time when you were bullied. First write what really happened. Then describe what you could have said and done to show the bully that you were strong, assertive and self-confident.

If you can't think of a time when you were bullied, make up a story in which you show a bully that you can't be pushed around.

A Book of Kindness

Purpose:
Kindness is an attribute that can be directly fostered and is an important antidote to bully behavior. By describing kind acts they did or received, students are reinforcing this positive behavior within themselves.

Materials:
writing materials; drawing paper; colored marking pens, crayons, or pencils; glue; a large three-ring binder

Procedure:
Write the word *kindness* on the board. Ask the students to help you define its meaning. In the process, make these points about kindness:
- Kindness is a quality that is developed from being kind.
- Being kind means being considerate, thoughtful, or helpful.
- An act of kindness is something you do. It is a deed or behavior. It's possible to have kind thoughts and feelings, but they are private until you express them in an act of kindness.
- A kind act is always done voluntarily, not because it is required.

Ask the students to brainstorm examples of kind acts. List their suggestions on the board. Encourage a variety of ideas, by asking questions like "What are some kind acts you can do for a friend? ...a classmate? ...brother or sister? ...parent? ...neighbor? ...your teacher? ...grandparent? ...a stranger? ...the environment? Include things like:
— make friends with a new student
— offer to share things
— talk to or play with kids who seem left out
— give someone a compliment
— read a story to a younger child
— visit senior citizens in a retirement or rest home
— help a friend do his/her chores
— help a classmate solve a tough math problem

— stand up for someone who is being bullied.
— surprise your parent by doing an "extra" chore at home
— hold a door for someone
— pick up trash when you see it lying around

Tell the students that you want them to write about and draw an act of kindness they've done — or one that someone else has done for them. Distribute writing and drawing materials. In your own words, explain:

"Describe the kind act, tell who did it, and for whom it was done. You don't have to mention names, just use words like 'friend,' 'teacher,' 'sister,' or 'older person.' Then write about the feelings of the person who did the kind deed, and the feelings of the person who received it. Draw a picture that shows the kind act being done."

As a final step, have the students assemble the story and drawing, either by writing a final version somewhere on the drawing itself, or by gluing the drawing to the story page, or vice-versa.

Have the students share their stories and pictures in small groups. Then place all of the finished work in the three-ring binder. Insert a cover page titled, "Book of Kindness." (Have one of the children illustrate the cover page.)

Discussion Questions:
1. Why is it important to try to turn kind thoughts into kind deeds?
2. When you have a kind thought about someone, how can you express it?
3. What are some specific ways we can show kindness here at school?
4. How do you feel when you commit a kind act?
5. If everyone in our class tried to do one kind act a day, how would our class benefit?

Two Sides of Friendship

Purpose:
Developing positive friendship skills is one of the most valuable things students can learn. Both bullies and targets generally lack the social skills to develop supportive, healthy friendships, which is a contributing factor to the bully or target roles they play.

Materials:
Experience Sheet, "What Is a Friend"
Three or more large pieces of butcher paper; masking tape; marking pens in assorted colors

Procedure:
Use the experience sheet as a prelude to this activity. Distribute the sheet and go over the directions. Give the students some examples of behaviors they might list on their sheets, then allow time for writing. When the students have finished, ask volunteers to share items from their lists.

Divide the students into small groups. Give a large piece of butcher paper and several markers to each group. Have each group select two members to start the activity. Give these directions:

One person lies down on the paper, assuming any position he or she wishes, and the other traces around that person's body with a marking pen to make a "person shape." When you have finished, turn the paper over and hand your markers to two other members of your group. The new pair will repeat the process using the reverse side of the paper.

Have the students label one side of the paper, "Things Good Friends Do," and the other side of the paper, "Things Friends Don't Do."

Have the groups tape their drawings to different walls around the room, with the "Things Good Friends Do" side up.

Direct the groups to brainstorm qualities that they value in a friend. These might include honesty, loyalty, good listening skills, friendliness, affection, helpfulness, and so forth. When a student has an idea, he or she must pick up a marking pen, go up to the drawing, and write the idea inside the person outline. At the same time, the student is to explain the idea to the rest of the group. Encourage all group members to get involved.

Circulate and stimulate discussion within each group. Get the students to focus on the values they are expressing. For example, say, "Cindy, you mentioned that you value being friendly. Would you please explain what that means to you? Jack, you and Lu both said friends are always honest. How do you feel if a friend lies to you?"

When the groups have finished filling in their person shapes, have them turn the paper over and use the other side to record qualities they do not value in a friend. These might include lying, tattling, backbiting, pressuring, name-calling and put downs. Encourage the students to think of their own experiences and fill up the drawing with ideas.

Have each group share its completed drawing (front and back) with the entire class. Facilitate discussion.

Discussion Questions:
1. What ideas were recorded by all three groups?
2. What ideas did you get from the drawings that you hadn't considered before? What are your thoughts about those ideas?
3. How will you use what you learned during this activity in your own friendships?

Extension:
Challenge the students to use some of the ideas generated during this activity to make a new friend or strengthen an existing friendship. In two weeks, ask volunteers to share their experiences.

What Is a Friend?

List the things that help to make good friendships.

List the things that can hurt a friendship.

Put a check mark beside the things you have done to make or keep a friend.

Put an X beside the things you have done that have hurt a friendship.

Setting Friendship Goals

Purpose:
This activity asks students to identify what they and others like about their friendship behaviors, ways to decrease negative friendship behaviors, and ways to increase positive ones. The students then formulate a goal and plan for improving one friendship behavior.

Materials:
Experience Sheet, "Becoming a Better Friend"
board or chart paper

Procedure:
Begin by reminding the students of the previous discussion concerning friendship. Announce that, today, the students are going to concentrate on evaluating their own friendship behaviors.

Ask several volunteers to name things they could begin doing (or stop doing) that would make them a better friend. List ideas on the board, such as:
- Learn how to start a conversation with a new person.
- Volunteer to help someone study for a test.
- Reach out to someone of a different race or cultural background.
- Include someone with a disability in my activities.
- Invite someone to eat lunch with me.
- Help a friend learn a new skill or game.
- Stick up for my friends (be loyal).
- Learn how to settle conflicts and negotiate differences.
- Practice giving compliments.
- Smile and use good eye contact when talking with others.
- Bring together friends from different groups in some common pursuit.

Ask the students to name behaviors that others respond to positively, as well as some that seem to turn others off. Offer examples from your own experience. You might say, "My positive friendship behaviors are that I always do what I say I'm going to do, so my friends can count on me. In addition, I have a generally positive attitude. I smile a lot, and I try to remember to tell people when I like their work, or something they've done, or the way they look. A negative behavior I need to work on is letting my thoughts jump ahead during conversations, because when I jump ahead, I tend to interrupt the person who is speaking."

Continue taking examples from the group until you think the students have the idea. Then distribute both pages of the experience sheet, "Becoming a Better Friend." Go over the directions, answering any questions. Allow the students time to complete the sheet.

Have the students pair up. Instruct the partners to take turns sharing three positive behaviors and one negative behavior, as you did in your earlier example. Suggest that they select from their experience sheet those behaviors they would most like to discuss. Allow about 5 minutes for sharing, signaling the partners at the halfway point.

Get the attention of the pairs, and take a few moments to talk about the importance of goals in changing behavior. Point out that no one is born knowing how to make and keep friends; rather, these behaviors are learned. When behaviors are learned, they can also be changed. Change involves setting goals for new behaviors and implementing step-by-step plans for achieving those goals.

Give the partners an additional 5 to 10 minutes to share their goals and action plans. Suggest that they help each other formulate steps for achieving their goals. Urge them to make a mutual contract to support each other through continued informal sharing and discussion over the next few weeks. Lead a culminating class discussion.

Discussion Questions:

1. How do you explain the fact that some people have so many friends and others have so few?
2. Why are friendships important? What do we gain from having friends?
3. Which was easier, naming positive friendship behaviors or naming negative friendship behaviors? Why?
4. What kinds of help and support do you need to really pursue your friendship goal? How and from whom will you get that help and support?

Becoming a Better Friend

Friends are important! If you could take three people with you on a trip around the world, whom would you take? Why?

Name	Reason
1.	
2.	
3.	

Keep it growing! Do you have a friendship with someone that just keeps getting better? What have you done to keep it growing?

_____
_____

What do you value in your friends? Complete this statement: People can show their friendship for me by...

_____
_____

Name five of your own friendship behaviors that others seem to like.

1. _____
2. _____
3. _____
4. _____
5. _____

Name two friendship behaviors that *seem* to turn others off.

1. _____
_____

2. _____
_____

To achieve your goal, you need a PLAN—a systematic way of putting your goal into action. What are *some* of the first steps you will take?

Think of one way in which you would like to improve your friendship behaviors. Write your GOAL here.

_____
_____
_____
_____
_____
_____
_____

Step 1: _____
_____

Step 2: _____
_____

Step 3: _____
_____

Step 4: _____
_____

Step 5: _____
_____

> Don't walk in front of me—
> I may not follow.
> Don't walk behind me—
> I may not lead.
> Walk beside me and
> just be my friend.
>
> —Camus

No Room for Bullies

Purpose::
Many young people are not equipped to deal with bully encounters, either as the target or as bystanders. This activity covers specific actions that can be taken to prevent being a target or to help bystanders to become upstanders.

Materials:
Experience sheet, "No Room for Bullies"; writing materials

Procedure:
On the board write "What Bullies Do." Tell the students that they have 5 minutes to write anything that comes to mind about this subject. Urge them to record a free flow of thoughts, ideas, and feelings.

When 5 minutes have elapsed, call time. Invite the students to share their ideas. Allow the contributions of the students to generate a group discussion.

Next, repeat the free-writing assignment, using the topic "How to Stop a Bully." Again, facilitate sharing and discussion.

At the conclusion of the activity and after asking the discussion questions, pass out a copy of the experience sheet, "No Room for Bullies," to each student. Review with the students the suggestions under both topics. Ask them to fill in any additional ideas they got from this activity at the bottom of the sheet. Encourage the students to keep the experience sheet and to read it often so they can remember what to do if they are bullied or see someone else being bullied.

Discussion Questions:
1. What similarities did you hear in the ideas we had about what bullies do?
2. What similarities and differences did you notice in our ideas about how to stop a bully?
3. Did anything stand out as very different?
4. Which topic was easier to respond to, what bullies do or how to stop a bully? Why do you think that was?
5. What ideas do you now have for stopping bully behavior?

No Room for Bullies

What To Do If You Are Bullied

- DON'T SHOW ANGER. It only makes matters worse and the bully will feel like he or she has control over you.
- DON'T FIGHT BACK. This lets the bully know you are angry and often it just leads to more force.
- WALK AWAY. Don't react. Just stand tall, confidently walk away, and ignore the bully.
- USE DISTRACTION. If you can't walk away, try saying something funny. Not about the bully but about yourself, or tell a joke. Sometimes this can distract a bully and throw them off guard.
- STAY WITH OTHERS. Don't be alone where a bully can harass you.
- ASK FOR HELP. Always tell a trusted adult if you are being bullied. Being bullied is not your fault, and you don't have to handle it alone.

Other Ideas:

_____
_____
_____
_____
_____

What To Do If You See Someone Being Bullied

- BE AN UPSTANDER NOT JUST A BYSTANDER. Tell the bully that their behavior is wrong and unacceptable. When you speak up it gives others confidence to do the same.
- IF YOU CAN, GET THE TARGET AWAY FROM THE BULLY.
- LET THE TARGET KNOW YOU CARE. Spend time talking with the target and listen to what he or she is feeling.
- INCLUDE THE TARGET IN ACTIVITIES. Sit together at lunch, or on the bus. Walk home from school together.
- ALWAYS TELL A TRUSTED ADULT ABOUT ANY BULLY INCIDENT YOU WITNESS. You are not tattling, but you are helping someone stay safe.

Other Ideas:

_____
_____
_____
_____
_____

Bringing It All Together

Purpose:
The students have developed increased awareness of bullying, and have been introduced to and practiced bully-handling skills. This last activity provides an opportunity for the students to review what they have learned and identify areas in which they still need help.

Materials:
Experience Sheet, "How to Handle a Bully"

Procedure:
Engage the students in a review of the bullying information that has been covered by the group. If you have any charts or displays remaining from previous lessons, take another look at them. Write the following list on the board to stimulate recall and help guide discussion:
- Different forms of bullying
- What motivates bullies, and the "masks" they wear
- The "Kids Bill of Rights"
- The importance of asking for help
- How to be an upstander not just a bystander
- How to report bullying incidents
- How to avoid bullies
- Positive self-talk and affirmations
- Assertiveness skills
- Relaxation strategies
- Handling anger
- The "standing tall" formula
- The "say no and go" formula
- How to make and keep friends

Encourage the students to comment on what they have learned, and ask review questions to stimulate discussion.

Review Questions:
1. What are some of the different ways that people bully others? (teasing, name-calling, hitting, gossip, exclusion, making fun of, force of any kind)
2. What are bullies trying to gain? (attention, power)
3. What are your rights, and how does knowing them help you?
4. When should you ask for help?
5. Whom should you tell if you are bullied or see someone else bullied?
6. What can you do to support a target and be an upstander?
7. What are some ways to avoid bullies?
8. How can positive self-talk defend you against bullies?
9. What is a positive self-talk statement or affirmation that you can say to yourself to feel strong and unafraid?
10. What is the difference between being assertive and being passive?
11. What is the difference between being assertive and being aggressive?
12. What formula did you learn for standing tall in a bully encounter? (Reach for the sky.)
13. What's another formula that you can say to yourself? (Say no and go.)
14. What did you learn about making and keeping friends?

Following the discussion, distribute the experience sheet. Explain the directions. Give the students plenty of time to list the things that they have learned and the things they still need help with. Circulate and provide assistance to individual students. Finally, encourage the students ask for adult help with anything that still puzzles or worries them.

How to Handle a Bully

You have learned a lot about bullies and how to handle them. Think about all the stories you have written, pictures you have drawn, and other activities you have done.

In the space below, list the ideas that you have learned and plan to use in the future — Things I have learned:

_____
_____
_____
_____
_____
_____
_____

Now list the things that you are still unsure of, or have questions about — Things I still need help with:

_____
_____
_____
_____
_____
_____
_____

Remember, it is important to ask for help when you need it. If anything (or anyone) is bothering you, go to an adult for help. You don't have to face a bully on your own.

Sharing Circle Topics

Something About Me That You Wouldn't Know Unless I Told You

Introducing the Topic:

Our topic for this session is, "Something About Me That You Wouldn't Know Unless I Told You." Can you curl your tongue or speak another language? Did you break your arm when you were five, or find a ten dollar bill once in the street? Have you been in another country? This is a chance for you to think of something that makes you special. Don't say anything that causes you to feel uncomfortable, just something that you would like to share about yourself that we might not know. Let's think about it quietly for a minute before sharing. The topic is, "Something About Me That You Wouldn't Know Unless I Told You."

Invite the children to take turns speaking, and encourage them to listen to each speaker carefully. Keep it positive and take a turn yourself.

Discussion Questions:
— Why do you think it is helpful to share with others things that they might not know about you?
— What does it mean to be unique? What are some different ways in which we are unique?

Someone Tried to Make Me Do Something I Didn't Want to Do

Introducing the Topic:

Today's topic has long been a favorite of students in the circle because it has happened to so many of them. The topic today is, "Someone Tried to Make Me Do Something I Didn't Want to Do." Maybe you can think of a time when someone you knew—perhaps a friend or a group of friends—wanted you to go some place or do something against your better judgment. Maybe you thought it might be harmful to you or someone else, or maybe it was illegal, or perhaps someone tried to get you to tease and bully another kid which you knew wasn't right.

The thing to focus on here is how you handled the situation. Did you go along with the person? If you did, how did you feel about it later? If you decided not to go along, how did you feel about that? Did it have any effect on your relationship with the person? This sort of situation can be very tough to handle; when it happens, we feel put on the spot. If you decide to share your experience, tell us what happened and how you felt, but don't tell us who was pressuring you. The topic today is, "Someone Tried to Make Me Do Something I Didn't Want to Do."

Discussion Questions:

1. What makes situations like this seem like no-win situations?
2. Which matters more—doing what you believe is right or shielding other people from disappointment?
3. Have you observed or learned anything of interest to you in this session that you would like to mention?

How Someone Made Me Feel Like Part of the Group

Introduce the topic:

Today our topic is, "How Someone Made Me Feel Like Part of the Group." Most of us have had the experience of being an outsider. Usually this happens when we are new to an area or school or are different in some way from most of the other people. Most of us probably don't like the uncomfortable feeling of being left out and of wanting to be included. Think of a time when you felt this way and someone took the time to get to know you, introduced you to the group and made you feel welcome. That person was your ticket to being "in." Maybe it happened at a club meeting or a dance. Or perhaps you were living in a new neighborhood or had just enrolled in a new school. Describe the specific situation, and tell us about the person who made you feel welcome and wanted. Our topic is, "How Someone Made Me Feel Like Part of the Group."

Discussion Questions:

1. What kinds of behaviors help people feel accepted?
2. How would you go about helping someone feel like part of your group?
3. How does it affect a group or organization when members really identify with the group and feel like they belong?

A Time I Was Rejected Because Something About Me Was Different

Introduce the topic:

Our topic for today's session is "A Time I Was Rejected Because Something About Me Was Different." Our purpose for discussing this topic is to find out how things like this happen and to talk about how it feels to be left out or turned away for something that you can't or won't change. So think of a time when this happened to you. What was it about you that led to the rejection? Was it the color of your skin? Were you too tall or not tall enough? Perhaps your clothing was unacceptable to the person or group who rejected you. Or maybe it was your weight, language or a disability. If you decide to share, tell us what happened without telling us who rejected you. The topic is, "I Was Rejected Because Something About Me Was Different."

Discussion Questions:

1. How are people affected when they are rejected for something about them that's different?
2. Why are we afraid or suspicious of differences among people?
3. What can we do to become more accepting of differences?

A Time I Felt Left Out

Introduce the Topic:

The topic for this session is, "A Time I Felt Left Out." At one time or another, all of us have been left out of something that we wanted to be included in. Maybe you were left out of a game the other kids were playing because they thought you weren't good enough, or perhaps your family wouldn't let you participate in a project because they decided you were too young. Maybe you weren't feeling well and couldn't go to school on the day of a big field trip. Or maybe your friends were invited to a birthday party and you weren't. Perhaps you were excluded from an activity because you use a wheelchair, couldn't throw a ball, were overweight, or are black. Whatever the reason was, you felt left out of what others were doing. Think about it for a few moments. The topic is, "I Time I Felt Left Out."

Discussion Questions

1. How did most of us feel about being left out?
2. Why is it so important to feel included?
3. What could you have done to be included?
4. Why do people exclude others from their activities?
5. What can you do if you see that someone else is being left out?

I Did Something That Made Me Feel Like a Good Person

Introducing the Topic:

Our Sharing Circle topic today is, "I Did Something That Made Me Feel Like a Good Person." We do many things that cause us to feel good about ourselves. Sometimes we do them spontaneously (on the spur of the moment) and sometimes we plan them in advance. Tell us about something you did that resulted in positive feelings. You may have done it for yourself, or for another person—or perhaps it was for an animal or the environment. Other people may have known about what you did, or you may have kept it to yourself until now. Think about it for a few moments. The topic is, "I Did Something That Made Me Feel Like a Good Person."

Discussion Questions:

1. When we feel we have done something good, is it important to get recognition from someone else? Why or why not?
2. How can you encourage yourself to do more good things so that your positive feelings will spread to other parts of your life?

A Time I Felt Anger and Handled It Well

Introduce the Topic:

Anger is one of the hardest emotions to deal with. It doesn't feel good and it's hard to control. In this session, we're going to talk about successfully controlling anger. Our topic is, "A Time I Felt Anger and Handled It Well."

Think of a time when you were angry at something or someone, but you bit your lip, or counted to ten, or did something else to keep from blowing up. You may have been mad at a friend, parent, teacher, brother or sister, and it could have been over something important or a tiny thing. Tell us what happened and what you did to control yourself, but please don't mention any names. The topic is, "A Time I Felt Anger and Handled It Well."

Discussion Questions:

1. Why is it important to control anger? What kinds of things can anger lead to if it isn't controlled?
2. What are some ways to let anger out, like air from a balloon, without actually getting angry?
3. What have you learned about anger from this session?
4. If you can learn to handle strong emotions like anger, how can that help you to handle other feelings and emotions?

A Way I Show I'm a Good Friend

Introducing the Topic:

Our topic for this session is, "A Way I Show I'm a Good Friend." There are many things we can do to demonstrate that we are a good friend. We can be helpful and supportive all the time, and we can do special things on special occasions. How do you show your friendship? Maybe you show it in the way you handle disagreements, or offer to help when your friend is in a jam. Maybe it's something as simple as being a good listener. Think about the things you do for your friends. When you're ready to share, the topic is, "A Way I Show I'm a Good Friend."

Discussion Questions:

1. What are some similarities and differences in the ways we show we're a good friend?
2. Why is it important to actively show that you're a good friend?
3. How do you feel when you are being a good friend?

A Friend I Have Who Is Different From Me

Introduce the Topic:

Today we're going to talk about our friends, particularly the ones who are different from us in some significant way. Our topic is, "A Friend I Have Who Is Different From Me."

Tell us about a friend of yours who is either much older or much younger, is of a different race or culture, or is very different from you in some other way. Tell us how you became friends with this person and what you like about him or her. I'll give you a few moments to decide what you want to share. Our topic is, "A Friend I Have Who Is Different From Me."

Discussion Questions:

1. What were the reasons we gave for liking these friends and valuing their friendship?
2. What, if any, problems or conflicts have been caused by the difference between you and your friend, and how have you handled them?
3. What have you and your friend been able to learn from each other as a result of your differences?
4. What is more important between friends, the things you have in common or your differences? Why?

Something Nice I Did For a Friend

Introduce the Topic:

Our topic for this session is, "Something Nice I Did for a Friend." Friends do thoughtful things for each other all the time. That's part of what builds friendship. Tell us something that you did for one of your friends. It doesn't have to be something spectacular — small deeds are important, too. For example, maybe you accompanied your friend to the library and helped her find some books for a report. Perhaps you offered to feed your friend's pet while he was on vacation. Or maybe you were a good listener when your friend was feeling sad or upset about something. Have you ever drawn a picture or made a little gift for a friend? Have you ever given a friend a funny card? There are many thoughtful things we can do for our friends. Tell us about one. The topic is, "Something Nice I Did for a Friend."

Discussion Questions:

1. How did you feel when you did the thoughtful thing you described?
2. How do you feel when your friends do nice things for you?
3. Why is it important to take the time to give thoughtful service to others?

I Told Someone How I Was Feeling

Introducing the Topic:

Our topic today is, "I Told Someone How I Was Feeling." Have you ever come right out and told someone how you were feeling about him or her? Think of a time you were very open in this way. Perhaps you were feeling joyful or amused at something the person did and you wanted him or her to know it. Perhaps you expressed strong negative feelings, like anger or resentment, in response to something the person did.

How did the person react? Was he or she pleased, respectful, surprised, angry, or defensive? What happened as a result of your openness? Think it over for a minute, and tell us about a time you were forthright in expressing your feelings. The topic is, "I Told Someone How I Was Feeling."

Discussion Questions:

1. Why do we sometimes hesitate to tell others our feelings?
2. When is it generally a good idea to tell people how you feel? When is it generally not a good idea?
3. How does it make you feel when someone really listens to you?
4. How do you feel about the person listening to you?

A Time I Listened Well to Someone

Introducing the Topic:

Most of us appreciate having someone really listen to us. In this session we are going to turn this idea around and talk about how it feels to listen to someone else. The topic is, "A Time I Listened Well to Someone."

Can you remember a time when you really paid attention to someone and listened carefully to what he or she said? This means that you didn't interrupt with your own ideas or daydream about your own plans, but really concentrated and tried to understand what the other person was attempting to get across. Maybe you've listened to a friend like that, or a younger brother or sister, or a teacher or coach. Think about it for a few moments and, if you wish, tell us about, "A Time I Listened Well to Someone."

Discussion Questions:

1. What kinds of things make listening difficult?
2. Why is it important to listen to others?
3. What could you do to improve your listening?
4. How do you feel when someone really listens to you?
5. How do you think the target of a bully would feel if you listened to how he or she was feeling?

How I Let Others Know I'm Interested In What They Say

Introduce the Topic:

Our topic for this session is, "How I Let Others Know I'm Interested in What They Say." One way we can let another person know that we are listening and interested in what they have to say is by what we say in response. There are many other things we can do, too. Some of these involve our posture, the way we make eye contact, or whether and how frequently we interrupt them. Think of some of the ways you show other people that you are interested in what they are saying. Also think about how you feel when others listen to you with interest. Select one of the ways that you show interest and tell us about it. Our topic is, "How I Let Others Know I'm Interested In What They Say."

Discussion Questions:

1. How do you think people feel knowing that you are really interested in what they have to say?
2. How do you feel knowing that others are interested in what you have to say?
3. What can you do to become a more effective listener and communicator?
4. Why is good listening so important?

Something About Me That's Likable and Worthy of Respect

Introduce the Topic:

Each of you is a unique person with many wonderful qualities — qualities that people like and respect. Today we're going to give ourselves credit for some of those qualities. Our topic is, "Something About Me That's Likable and Worthy of Respect."

What is one quality, characteristic, or trait in yourself that you are particularly proud of? Maybe you are a very friendly person, or helpful, or a hard worker. Perhaps people respect the fact that you are reliable, and always keep your promises and commitments. Or maybe your sense of humor is particularly likable. Are you loyal to your friends and family? Are you an understanding, sympathetic, compassionate person? Are you honest and trustworthy? Are you smart, sensible, or logical? Think about your many good qualities for a few moments and tell us about one of them. The topic is, "Something About Me That's Likable and Worthy of Respect."

Discussion Questions:

1. How do you feel when talking about your best qualities?
2. Why is it important to recognize good qualities in ourselves?
3. What does it mean to respect someone?
4. Is it possible to have a trait or quality that is likable, but not respectable? What about respectable, but not likable? Explain.

How I Show Respect Toward Others

Introduce the Topic:

Our topic today is about <u>showing</u> respect, which is not the same as <u>having</u> respect. When you have respect for someone, you feel it inside; when you show respect, your actions demonstrate it. Our topic is, "How I Show Respect Toward Others."

Maybe you show your respect for people by being courteous and polite. Another way to show respect is to listen attentively when a person talks and not ridicule or make fun of what he says. Facial expressions can show respect or the lack of it; so can posture, gestures, and other types of body language. At times, showing respect can also mean leaving a person alone, not bothering her, allowing her to believe in, talk about, and do what she thinks is right for her. You might want to picture in your mind someone whom you respect and then think about how you act toward that person that shows your respect. Our topic is, "How I Show Respect Toward Others."

Discussion Questions:

1. What respectful actions were mentioned most during our circle?
2. How do you feel when someone shows respect for you?
3. Why is it important to demonstrate our respect for others?
4. What is the difference between having respect and showing it?
5. Who decides how you will act toward another person?

What's Good and Bad About Peer Pressure

Introduce the Topic:

Usually we think of peer pressure as a bad thing — kids pressuring each other to do things like use drugs, join gangs, or bully someone. But today, we're going to talk about both sides of peer pressure, because there is a good side, too. Our topic is, "What's Good and Bad About Peer Pressure."

Tell us one thing that you think is bad about peer pressure, but also share one positive thing. If possible, draw from experiences with your own friends, but don't mention names. For example, maybe your peers have pressured you to take good risks, like running for school office or trying out for a team. On the other hand, they might have pressured you to take bad risks, like doing stunts on your skateboard that you're not skilled enough to do, or going somewhere after school that your parents have said is off limits. Peers can pressure you to use tobacco, alcohol, bad language, drugs, and to do lots of other undesirable things, but they can also pressure you to stay fit, dress nicely, use good manners, and participate in worthwhile activities. Take a minute to think about it. Our topic is, "What's Good and Bad About Peer Pressure."

Discussion Questions:
1. Who makes the final decision about what you will do and won't do?
2. Why is peer pressure so hard to resist?
3. What goes through your mind when you are deciding whether to go along with peer pressure or not?

A Time I Stood Up for What Was Right

Introduce the Topic:

Today we're going to talk about situations that require courage, the courage to do what is right when our companions are doing — or are about to do — something wrong. Our topic is, "A Time I Stood Up for What Was Right."

Think about situations in which you were with other people — kids or family members — and something happened that caused you to take a stand. Maybe a friend wanted to do something dishonest or hurtful, and you refused to be involved. Perhaps some kids wanted to go somewhere that was unsafe or off-limits, and you talked them out of it. Or maybe you convinced a friend, or a brother or sister, to tell the truth instead of lying. Without mentioning any names, tell us what happened and how you felt. The topic is, "A Time I Stood Up for What Was Right."

Discussion Questions:

1. What is courage? How did we get up our courage in the situations we talked about?
2. How do you feel inside when you stand up for the right thing?
3. How were the other people in our examples better off because we took a stand? How did they benefit?

I Stopped Myself from Damaging Someone's Property

Introduce the Topic:

Today, our topic is about vandalism, which is the act of damaging another person's property. We're going to discuss times when we came close to being vandals ourselves. The topic is, "I Stopped Myself from Damaging Someone's Property."

Can you remember a time when you almost did something to a person's property that would have made it less valuable or worthless, but stopped yourself? A person's property is any possession — a coat, book, bike, paper, pencil, game, house, car, yard, furniture, or anything else that belongs to the person. Maybe you were angry at someone and you were tempted to get even by damaging something belonging to the person. Or perhaps you were with some friends and came close to participating in an act of vandalism because the group pressured you to "join in." Tell us what happened and what caused you to change your mind. Take a few moments to think it over. The topic is, "I Stopped Myself from Damaging Someone's Property."

Discussion Questions:

1. Why is it wrong to damage or hurt in any way another person's things?
2. Has anyone ever damaged a possession of yours? How did you feel?
3. What can you do if your friends are pressuring you to do something you know is wrong?

Someone Who Trusts Me

Introducing the Topic:

Our topic for this session is, "Someone Who Trusts Me." All of us experience many feelings in our lives. Some are good feelings, and some are bad. Sometimes, we tend to take the good feelings for granted; we fail to appreciate them, or even forget about them completely. An example is the good feeling we have when someone trusts us.

Think of someone who trusts you, and how that trust makes you feel. This is someone who feels good enough about you and what you are capable of doing that he or she believes in you wholeheartedly. This is probably someone who likes to have you around, and who doesn't find it necessary to question or check up on you very much. This "someone" could be a parent, friend, relative, teacher—even an pet. Take a minute to think about it, and then let's discuss, "Someone Who Trusts Me."

Discussion Questions:

1. Do you find that you usually trust people who trust you? Why or why not?
2. Why do you think the person you talked about trusts you?
3. What kinds of qualities and behaviors tend to earn the trust of others?

Someone I Would Like to Know Better

Introducing the Topic:

Today's Sharing Circle topic is, "Someone I Would Like to Know Better." We interact with many people every day. Some are friends. Others are acquaintances. Still others are strangers. Occasionally, we meet someone whom we wish we could know better. Has this ever happened to you?

Maybe the person you'd like to know better is a relative you see only occasionally at family gatherings. Maybe he or she is a classmate who sits across the room, or who shares only one class with you, or it's a new kid in school. Maybe the person you'd like to know is a celebrated athlete, actor, politician, or business executive. Or perhaps you simply want to spend time getting to know you grandparents better so that you can understand and appreciate all the things they've seen and accomplished in life. Think about it for a few moments. Our topic is, "Someone I Would Like to Know Better."

Discussion Questions:

1. What can you do to get to know someone better?
2. What obstacles can prevent us from getting to know new people?
3. What qualities in a person make you want to know him or her?

Something I Like About Myself Right Now

Introducing the Topic:

Today's Sharing Circle topic is, "Something I Like About Myself Right Now." You could respond in many ways to this topic. Maybe you like some physical part of you, like your hair or the freckles on your nose. Perhaps what you like is that you are studying hard and doing well in a particular subject. Maybe you like the way you recently handled a tough problem, or how you are relating to a friend.

Really think about this for a minute, and identify something that is currently giving you a good feeling about yourself. If you decide to share, tell us what you like about yourself and how it makes you feel inside. Our topic is, "Something I Like About Myself Right Now."

Discussion Questions:

1. Is it easy or difficult to talk about yourself in a positive way? Explain.
2. Why is it important to have positive feelings about yourself?
3. How can you expand your positive beliefs about yourself to other areas?

It Made Me Feel Good to Make Someone Else Feel Good

Introducing the Topic:

The topic today is, "It Made Me Feel Good to Make Someone Else Feel Good." When we contribute to good feelings in others, we usually feel good ourselves. In fact, we sometimes benefit as much as the recipient. Think of a time when you enjoyed positive feelings by making someone else feel good.

Maybe you helped a new student find a classroom, or went out of your way to compliment someone's appearance. Perhaps you helped someone understand a difficult math concept, or taught a new player how to pitch a curve ball. You may have stood up for someone who was being bullied or teased. Or you may have helped an elderly neighbor carry groceries. Tell us about one time when you helped another person feel good and in the process felt good yourself. The topic is, "It Made Me Feel Good to Make Someone Else Feel Good."

Discussion Questions:

1. Why do we feel good when we help someone else feel good?
2. What sort of planning is required to make someone feel good?
3. What would this school be like if we all spent a little more time helping others feel good?

How Somebody Hurt My Feelings

Introducing the Topic:

Today we are going to talk about, "How Somebody Hurt My Feelings." Our feelings get hurt in many ways. Frequently, we feel hurt because of something that someone else did. The person who hurt us may not even realize the effects of his or her actions. Can you think of a time when someone hurt you?

Maybe a friend didn't invite you to a party or ignored you when you wanted to talk. Perhaps someone called you a name, or said something rude to you. Maybe a coach cut you from a team, or a teacher reprimanded you harshly in front of other students. Choose a time when your feelings were hurt. Tell us what happened and how you felt, but please don't mention any names. The topic is, "How Somebody Hurt My Feelings."

Discussion Questions:

1. What kinds of things tend to hurt our feelings most?
2. What are some ways we can cope with hurt feelings?
3. What role do our expectations play in whether or not we feel hurt?

I Could Have Hurt Someone's Feelings, But I Didn't

Introducing the Topic:

Today our topic is, "I Could Have Hurt Someone's Feelings, But I Didn't." We have all been in situations where we could have said or done something to hurt another person. This sort of opportunity presents itself frequently, for a variety of reasons. Think about a time when you were in this position. Maybe someone said or did something that wasn't appropriate, and you could easily have corrected or criticized the person, but for some reason you decided against it. Perhaps you heard someone exaggerate or lie in order to impress people, but you decided not to let on that you knew the truth. Or when someone made an embarrassing mistake, perhaps you bit your tongue and didn't laugh. Your decision might have been based on friendship, or fear that the person might hurt you back, or your realization that what the person was going through at that moment wasn't easy. Think about an experience you've had like this and, without telling us who the person was, share what happened. Our topic is, "I Could Have Hurt Someone's Feelings, But I Didn't."

Discussion Questions:

1. What were some of the things that kept us from hurting other people's feelings?
2. How did you feel about yourself for making the choice not to hurt someone's feelings?
3. What was the most important thing you learned in this session?

A Time I Stood Up for Something I Strongly Believe In

Introducing the Topic:

Today's topic is, "A Time I Stood Up for Something I Strongly Believe In." Most of us have experienced at least once the necessity to take a stand concerning something. Standing up for a belief can be difficult, especially if friends or relatives do not agree with us. Even when they do agree, it is not necessarily easy to state our beliefs publicly. Think of a time when this happened to you.

Maybe you saw others doing something that you felt was wrong, and you confronted them. Perhaps you were involved in a discussion about a controversial subject, and you stated your views, even though they were unpopular. You may remember being nervous and worrying about the uncertainty of the situation. Or you may have felt very sure of yourself. Perhaps when you look back on the occasion, you recall a sense of pride, accomplishment, or even daring. If the outcome was different from what you wanted, tell us what you learned from the experience. Remember, don't mention any names. The topic is, "A Time I Stood Up for Something I Strongly Believe In."

Discussion Questions:

1. What similarities were there in our reasons for standing up for what we believe in?
2. When is it hardest for you to stand up for your beliefs?
3. What conditions enable you to stand up for what you believe in?
4. How do you feel about yourself when you stand up for your beliefs?

**If your heart is in
Social-Emotional Learning,
visit us online**

Come see us at
www.InnerchoicePublishing.com

Our web site gives you a look at all our other
Social-Emotional Learning-based books, free activities,
articles, research, and learning and teaching strategies.

Subscribe to our weekly blog, and every week you'll receive
a new activity or Sharing Circle topic and lesson.

INNERCHOICE Publishing
15079 Oak Chase Court
Wellington, FL 33414

www.InnerchoicePublishing.com

www.ingramcontent.com/pod-product-compliance
Lightning Source LLC
Chambersburg PA
CBHW081218230426
43666CB00015B/2785

www.ingramcontent.com/pod-product-compliance
Lightning Source LLC
Chambersburg PA
CBHW081218230426
43666CB00015B/2785